PASS Cambridge BEC Preliminary

Second Edition

Workbook with Answer Key

Ian Wood

PASS
Cambridge
BEC Preliminary

Second Edition

Workbook with Answer Key

Ian Wood

Summertown
Publishing

NATIONAL
GEOGRAPHIC
LEARNING

HEINLE
CENGAGE Learning·

Australia • Brazil • Japan • Korea • Mexico • Singapore • Spain • United Kingdom • United States

Pass Cambridge BEC Preliminary Workbook, Second Edition
Ian Wood

Publisher: Jason Mann

Senior Commissioning Editor: John Waterman

Editorial Project Manager: Karen White

Development Editor: Manuela Lima

Content Project Editor: Denise Power

Production Controller: Tom Relf

Marketing and Communications Manager: Michelle Cresswell

Head of Production and Manufacturing: Alissa McWhinnie

Compositor: MPS Limited, a Macmillan Company

Text Design: InPraxis

Cover Design: Maria Papageorgiou

ISBN-13: 978-1-133-31651-0

Heinle, Cengage Learning EMEA
Cheriton House, North Way, Andover, Hampshire, SP10 5BE
United Kingdom

Cengage Learning is a leading provider of customised learning solutions with office locations around the globe, including Singapore, the United Kingdom, Australia, Mexico, Brazil and Japan. Locate our local office at **international.cengage.com/region**

Cengage Learning products are represented in Canada by Nelson Education Ltd.

Visit Heinle at **http://elt.heinle.com**
Visit our corporate website at **www.cengage.com**

Printed in China by R.R Donnelley
1 2 3 4 5 6 7 8 9 10 – 17 16 15 14 13 12

Introduction

The Cambridge Business English Certificate

The Cambridge Business English Certificate (BEC) is an international Business English examination which offers a language qualification for learners who use, or will need to use, English for their work. It is available at three levels.

Level 1 Preliminary
Level 2 Vantage
Level 3 Higher

Cambridge BEC is a practical examination that focuses on English in business-related situations. The emphasis is on the development of language skills for work: reading, writing, listening and speaking.

Pass Cambridge BEC Preliminary

As an examination preparation course, *Pass Cambridge BEC Preliminary* focuses on the language skills tested at BEC Preliminary (reading, writing, listening and speaking) as well as the examination skills required to fully prepare students who wish to take the exam.

Pass Cambridge BEC Preliminary Workbook

As an important component of the *Pass Cambridge BEC Preliminary* course, the Workbook provides a language-focused supplement to the Student's Book. Each four-page unit is split into a grammar and a vocabulary section. Please note that there is no Workbook material for the Exam focus units of the Student's Book.

Pass Cambridge BEC Preliminary Workbook includes the following features.

- **Grammar**
  Each grammar section begins with a clear and full explanation of the grammar presented in the Student's Book. This is followed by extensive practice exercises that test and develop the student's knowledge. A full Answer key is provided at the back of the book.

- **Vocabulary**
  Each vocabulary section recycles key items from the *Pass Cambridge BEC Preliminary Student's Book* and introduces more key BEC Preliminary vocabulary. *Pass Cambridge BEC Preliminary Workbook* presents, revises and tests over 600 items of essential BEC Preliminary vocabulary. A full Answer key is provided at the back of the book.

- **Review**
  After every four units of the *Pass Cambridge BEC Preliminary Workbook,* there is a language review. Each review consists of fifty grammar questions, which revise the grammar of the previous four units, and fifty multiple-choice vocabulary questions also based on the previous four units. A full Answer key is provided at the back of the book.

- **Writing**
  This reference section provides students with guidance on writing emails and formal letters. The section includes a list of essential phrases useful to students not only in the examination but also in their professional lives.

Contents

		Grammar	Vocabulary

		Grammar	Vocabulary

Jobs

Present simple

Form   **The present simple has the following forms.**

I /you /we /they
*I **work** as a marketing manager.*
*We **don't sell** directly.*
***Do** you **deal** with the press?*

he /she /it
*He **interviews** the new applicants.*
*She **doesn't deal** with the staff.*
***Does** the job **involve** travelling?*

Use   **The present simple is used in the following ways.**

- to describe facts
*We **don't have** an office in France.*
*What **does** your company **produce**?*
- to describe permanent situations
*I **work** for Vacupak.*
*The company **employs** about 800 people.*
- to describe routines
*I **deal** with designers and printers every day.*
*My train **gets** in at seven forty-five.*

Note!   **Modal verbs (e.g. *can, could, will, would, might*) do not need auxiliary verbs.**

We ~~don't can find~~ the right candidate for the job.
*We **can't find** the right candidate for the job.*

Adverbs of frequency

Form   **Adverbs of frequency are used in the following ways.**

- before the verb (except *be*)
*I **usually** get the bus to work.*
*He doesn't **often** answer the phone.*
- after the verb *be*
*She's **always** the last to leave the office.*
*He's **never** late for work.*

Note!   **Adverbs of frequency can be used in other positions for emphasis.**

***Usually** I get the bus to work.*
*I get the bus to work **usually**.*
*~~I get **usually** the bus to work~~.*

Words such as *hourly, daily* and *weekly* go after the verb.

*We meet **weekly** to discuss sales.*
*The bonuses are paid **annually**.*

Grammar practice

Present simple

1 Complete the sentences with the correct form of the verbs in brackets.

1 She (work) ____works____ for an advertising agency.
2 I (check) _____ all the computer systems in the office.
3 The managers (spend) _____ a lot of time in meetings.
4 I (not / leave) _____ work before six o'clock most days.
5 The department (not / have) _____ a full-time secretary.
6 (you / work) _____ weekends?
7 My colleague (deal) _____ with all the orders.
8 (your job / involve) _____ much travelling?

2 Use the following words to write questions to the answers below.

~~what~~	how	who	where	how often	when	what kind of

1 I work as a <u>sales executive</u>. What do you do? _____
2 He works <u>in the Netherlands</u>. _____
3 I usually have lunch <u>at about 11.30</u>. _____
4 They use <u>Apple</u> computers at work. _____
5 She travels to work <u>by train</u>. _____
6 I report to the <u>Head of Department</u>. _____
7 My boss goes to Head Office <u>twice a month</u>. _____

Adverbs of frequency

3 Rearrange the words to make correct sentences.

1 works / one day a week / usually / from home / she
   She usually works from home one day a week. _____

2 rarely / receive / we / telephone calls
   _____

3 late / the bonuses / always / are
   _____

4 often / we / until 7.30 / the office / leave / don't
   _____

5 annually / in Prague / meet / all the managers
   _____

Present simple and adverbs of frequency

4 Find and correct the mistake in each line of the text. Tick (✓) any correct line.

1 My name is Karl-Heinz Egonolf. I <u>works</u> for a small management   ____work____
2 consultancy, which is based in Berlin. My job involve visiting   _____
3 companies and helping them improve their performance. I spend   _____
4 often several weeks at a company because I have to get to   _____
5 know the way the company work and what its problems are. A   _____
6 company sometimes knows not why it is performing badly. When   _____
7 I arrive at a new company, I look always very carefully at all of the   _____
8 company's accounts to see how it spend its money. Without this   _____
9 important information, I don't can give the client advice on how to   _____
10 cut costs and improve performance.   _____

Vocabulary practice

Job titles **1** **Use the clues below to find eighteen job titles in the puzzle.**

S	A	E	N	G	I	N	E	E	R	R	T
A	C	L	E	R	K	T	R	A	D	E	R
L	C	H	A	I	R	M	A	N	A	T	C
P	O	D	S	B	W	Y	M	P	C	E	O
A	U	D	I	T	O	R	N	O	R	R	N
R	N	R	O	R	F	U	R	R	E	P	S
T	T	O	C	J	E	E	R	T	K	R	U
S	A	O	P	H	Y	C	S	E	O	E	L
I	N	F	G	W	A	F	T	R	R	T	T
P	T	S	A	L	E	S	S	O	B	N	A
Y	O	L	D	H	T	U	E	K	R	I	N
T	S	E	C	R	E	T	A	R	Y	B	T

Find someone who …

1 ~~buys goods from suppliers~~
2 manages a company's finances
3 works with heavy machinery
4 approves a company's accounts
5 works in a restaurant kitchen
6 does hard manual work
7 looks after a company's legal affairs
8 types letters, answers the phone etc.
9 sits on the board of a company

10 works on the counter at a bank
11 heads the board of directors
12 assists a senior manager
13 types letters and reports
14 buys and sells stocks and shares
15 gives advice to companies
16 translates at international meetings
17 carries bags at a good hotel
18 buys and sells goods

Word formation **2** **Complete the table. Then use the words to complete the sentences below.**

person	verb	noun
trainer	train	training
operator	operate	_____
_____	_____	supervision
_____	assess	_____
co-ordinator	_____	_____
_____	_____	inspection

1 She's a good ___trainer___ . She did a great session on team-building last week.
2 A health and safety _____ is coming to see the factory tomorrow.
3 We've done an _____ of the investment we'll need to make next year.
4 Louise is responsible for the smooth _____ of the company website.
5 He's responsible for the _____ between the two departments.
6 Peter's going to _____ the new person for the first few weeks.

Terms and conditions

3 Look at the answers given to a candidate at a job interview. Match each one with one of the following topics. Not all of the topics are mentioned. Underline the words which helped you.

> trade union   pension   retirement   holidays   salary
> bonuses   illness   duties   working hours   workplace

1 Yes, we do have one here. I think about half of the workforce are members. A representative will approach you once you've started the job and talk to you about joining.

2 The basic contract has an allowance for twenty-five days a year. After several years with the company this will rise and some people even negotiate unpaid leave.

3 The company has a profit-sharing scheme. Of course, it does depend on the company having a good year but it usually pays about 3–5% of basic annual salary each year. It's open to full-time employees only.

4 Well, the official company policy is sixty-two for men and sixty for women but many of our employees leave early and some even work on past that age.

5 We have a company scheme for all our employees. You pay 5% of your gross annual salary and the company matches it. When you retire, you will then receive a proportion of your final salary each year, depending on your length of service.

6 We believe very strongly in rewarding our people with what they are worth so annual pay rises are negotiated on an individual basis, according to the employee's performance that year.

7 Employees are allowed up to three working days without having to produce a sick note. Of course, they are expected to phone in and report their absence to their line manager.

8 We work a system called 'flex', where employees are basically responsible for their own time-keeping. We do expect them to be in the office for most of the day, though, and to work the minimum requirement.

4 Say whether the following sentences are 'Right' or 'Wrong' according to the texts above. If there is not enough information to answer, write 'Doesn't say'.

1 The oldest worker in the company is sixty-two years old. _____
2 Employees can have more than twenty-five days' holiday a year. _____
3 All employees are part of the company's profit-sharing scheme. _____
4 The trade union has a good relationship with the management. _____
5 Employees receive a good monthly income when they retire. _____
6 Employees need a doctor's certificate if they have a day off work sick. _____
7 The company believes in giving large pay rises. _____
8 All employees finish work at the same time. _____

Companies

Past simple

Form The past simple has the following forms.

regular (with -ed)

We **started** business in 2002.
I **didn't start** work here until 2006.
When **did** you **start** exporting?

irregular

We **made** $20m profit in 2008.
They **didn't make** any profit until 2010.
How much profit **did** they **make**?

Use The past simple is used in the following ways.

* to describe finished events
  We **launched** the product in 2011.
  How **did** the conference **go**?

* to refer to finished time periods
  He **set up** the company in 1996.
  What **was** the hotel like in Shanghai? (The trip is finished.)

Note! **Past simple verbs are either regular (ending in -ed) or irregular.**
(See page 162 of the Student's Book for a list of irregular forms.)

Present continuous

Form The present continuous has the following forms.

I

I**'m staying** in the office today.
I**'m not working** tomorrow.
Who **am** I **speaking** to?

you / we / they

We**'re investing** heavily in Russia.
They **aren't making** any profit.
Are you **going** to the meeting?

He / she / it

She**'s going** to Brazil next week.
The company**'s doing** well right now.
Who**'s speaking**, please?

Use The present continuous is used in the following ways.

* to describe actions happening at the time of speaking (often with *at the moment, right now, just now*)
  We**'re investing** heavily in Guangzhou at the moment.

* to describe temporary situations
  Sales **aren't doing** very well just now.
  I**'m dealing** with the Swiss office for a few weeks.

* to refer to future arrangements
  We**'re going** to the marketing conference in July.
  When **are** you **travelling** to Norway?

Note! **We do not use the present continuous to express the following.**

routines *(usually, normally)*
opinions *(think, believe)*
senses *(see, hear, feel)*

emotions *(like, love, hate)*
ownership *(own, have, need)*

Grammar practice

Past simple **1** **Complete the text below with the correct form of the verbs in brackets.**

> ### The Founding of Nokia
>
> Nokia's history (¹begin) __began__ in 1865, when engineer Fredrik Idestam (²establish) _____ a wood-pulp mill by a riverbank in southern Finland and (³start) _____ manufacturing paper. The company, which he (⁴name) _____ Nokia, (⁵become) _____ successful as the consumption of paper and cardboard (⁶increase) _____ during European industrialisation. A large workforce (⁷come) _____ to the Nokia factory, and a town of the same name (⁸grow) _____ up around it.
>
> Nokia (⁹not/begin) _____ the journey into telecommunications until the 1960s when the company (¹⁰merge) _____ with the Finnish Cable Works. During the 1980s, Nokia's operations rapidly (¹¹expand) _____ into even more business sectors and countries. In 1988 Nokia (¹²be) _____ Europe's third-largest television manufacturer. In May 1992 the company (¹³appoint) _____ Jorma Ollila to head the whole of the Nokia Group. Nokia then (¹⁴make) _____ the strategic decision to focus on telecommunications. In February 2011, Nokia (¹⁵announce) _____ a partnership with Microsoft, which means most Nokia smartphones are now powered by the Windows operating system.

Present continuous **2** **Complete the dialogue with the correct form of the verbs in brackets.**

Peter   Hello, Sales Office.

Susan   Peter, it's Susan. I (¹call) ____'m calling____ from the exhibition.

Peter   Of course! How (²it / go) _____ ?

Susan   Very well. It (³get) _____ very busy right now.

Peter   That's great! (⁴you / sell) _____ anything?

Susan   No, we (⁵not / sell) _____ much, but it's still early. I guess our visitors (⁶look) _____ around the other stands first.

Peter   How long (⁷you / stay) _____ there today?

Susan   All day. I (⁸not / fly) _____ back until tomorrow.

Peter   So, (⁹you / attend) _____ the gala dinner this evening?

Susan   Of course. I (¹⁰look) _____ forward to it.

Peter   I'm sure you are! What is it, about seven courses and several different wines?

Susan   Yes, it's something like that. Look, Peter, I've got to go. There's a customer here and he (¹¹ask) _____ me a question.

Peter   OK. Bye Susan. And *bon appétit* this evening!

Present tenses **3 Choose the correct verb form to complete each sentence.**

1 We *invest* / *'re investing* heavily in Brazil at the moment.
2 The company *wants* / *is wanting* to break into the Chinese market.
3 They *have* / *'re having* a joint venture in India already.
4 We're an electronics company. We *manufacture* / *are manufacturing* radios.
5 The company usually *launches* / *is launching* its products in the autumn.
6 The board *doesn't believe* / *isn't believing* it's the right move just now.
7 We *take* / *'re taking* a big risk entering the market at this time.
8 When *do you go* / *are you going* to Yunnan?
9 I *think* / *'m thinking* an overseas production base could cut costs.
10 Although still lower than in the west, wages here *rise* / *are rising* steadily at the moment.

Past simple **4 Complete the sentences with the correct form of the verbs in brackets.**

1 The company (*not* / *become*) __didn't become__ a plc until 2010.
2 Communication with the subsidiary (*not* / *be*) _____ very good.
3 When (*they* / *set up*) _____ the joint venture?
4 The monopoly (*not* / *allow*) _____ for fair competition in the market.
5 Where (*you* / *locate*) _____ the first overseas production facility?
6 Why (*the bank* / *reject*) _____ the idea for an internet business?
7 They (*not* / *think*) _____ the joint venture would be successful.
8 Why (*they* / *not* /*stay*) _____ an independent company?

Vocabulary practice

Setting up a company **1 Match the verbs with the nouns then use them to complete the text below.**

research	equipment
recruit	the market
draw up	a profit
set up	a business plan
make	a company
locate	staff
invest in	funding
get	premises

Setting up a company

The very first thing we did was ¹research the market, which took us several months, looking at competitors and trying to find out what our customers would want. We then went to the bank to ² _____ . That was hard. At the first interview the bank told us to go away and ³ _____ so they could check all our figures and forecasts. We'd already found some empty office space so luckily we didn't have to ⁴ _____ . Before we could put job ads in the paper and ⁵ _____ , we had to make everything completely legal so we ⁶ _____ officially, which we did with the help of a solicitor. Finally, we had to ⁷ _____ and buy computers and office furniture. Of course, we realised it would be quite a while before we'd ⁸ _____ but we were still really excited about the thought of being our own bosses.

2 Match each headline with one of the following industries or sectors. Underline the words which helped you.

> agriculture   banking   leisure   manufacturing   retail   oil
> publishing   telecommunications   automobile

1 EU commissioner to rule on import car prices

2 Book sales hit by internet growth

3 High fuel costs leave many small farmers facing bankruptcy says report

4 Output down as factory gate prices fall in first quarter

5 Account holders still worried about online security

6 Indian mobile operators bid for next generation licences

Confusables   **3** Choose the correct word to complete each sentence.

1 The company has an annual *takeover* / *turnover* of $2m.
2 As a *retailer* / *wholesaler*, we only sell to the major supermarkets.
3 We had to buy a lot of new *plant* / *factory* for the new premises.
4 Our major *subsidy* / *subsidiary* in Mexico supplies the US market.
5 The discounts should give us a competitive advantage over our *rivals* / *partners*.
6 I work in the *Personnel* / *Personal* Department of a multinational.

Odd one out   **4** Which word is the odd one out?

1	trade mark	brand	factory	logo
2	break up	establish	set up	build
3	merger	alliance	partnership	monopoly
4	division	headquarters	factory	warehouse
5	marketing	personnel	agriculture	administration
6	funding	grant	finance	sales
7	run	manage	co-ordinate	produce
8	grow	expand	specialise	increase

Communication

Modal verbs

Form   **Modals are auxiliary verbs which show a speaker's attitude. There are nine modal verbs in English. (*Could* / *would* can be past forms of *can* / *will*.)**

can	*will*	*shall*	*may*	*must*
could	*would*	*should*	*might*	

Modal verbs do not take -s, *to* or the auxiliary *do*.

He cans understand Korean.
We should to phone again later.
I don't can do it by Friday. (I can't do it by Friday.)

Use   **Modal verbs are used in the following ways. Non-modal verbs with similar meanings are also given in the brackets.**

- to express intentions (*will, might* – also *going to*)
  *I'**ll put** them in the post today.*
  *I **won't do** anything until we get the figures.*
  *We **might get** a new scanner next month.*
  *We'**re going to upgrade** the computer network.*

- to express permission (*can, may* – also *be allowed to*)
  ***May* / *Can* I use** the phone, please?
  *We'**re allowed to send** personal emails.*

- to express ability (*can, could* – also *be able to*)
  *We **can do** it by Friday.*
  *Our old photocopier **isn't able to staple** copies.*

- to express obligation (*must, should* – also *have to*)
  *You **must** / **have to register** all the office software.*
  *You **should** password **protect** your computer.*

- to express prohibition (*mustn't, can't, shouldn't*)
  *You **mustn't** / **can't download** screensavers from the internet.*
  *You **shouldn't photocopy** from books.*

- to make offers (*will, shall, can*)
  *I'**ll arrange** a meeting for next week.*
  ***Shall* I email** it to you?
  ***Can* I help** you?

- to make suggestions (*should, shall, could*)
  *We **should** call the photocopier engineer.*
  ***Shall* we meet** on Wednesday?
  *We **could postpone** the meeting.*

- to make requests (*can, could, would, may*)
  ***Can* / *Could* / *Would* you translate** this for me?
  ***May* I have** a word with you?

Note!   ***Will* is used for spontaneous offers / decisions.**

I call you back later.
*I'**ll** call you back later.*

Grammar practice

Modal verbs   **1** **Choose the correct option to complete each sentence.**

1 PRINTERS MUST NOT BE LEFT ON OVERNIGHT

2 John
I'm afraid I won't manage to get the network up and running again today.
Susan

3 All prices are subject to change.

4 May we remind all staff to order any office equipment through Shelley.

1 Staff
  a) should switch printers off.
  b) can switch printers off.
  c) mustn't switch printers off.

2 Susan
  a) doesn't want to fix the network.
  b) isn't able to fix the network.
  c) shouldn't fix the network.

3 The company
  a) will change prices.
  b) might change prices.
  c) can't change prices.

4 Staff
  a) should order through Shelley.
  b) can order through Shelley.
  c) are allowed to order through Shelley.

2 **Complete the dialogue with the correct modal verbs.**

Sales Hello, Sales.
Jeff   Oh, hello. (¹*I /speak*) ___Can I speak___ to Göran Larson, please?
Sales I'm afraid Göran isn't here today. (²*I / help*) _____ ?
Jeff   (³*you / give*) _____ Göran a message for me?
Sales Sure. I (⁴*just / get*) _____ a pen. (⁵*I / ask*) _____ who's calling, please?
Jeff   It's Jeff Boisman from the Chicago office. (⁶*you / tell*) _____ him that I (⁷*not / make*) _____ our meeting in Stockholm on Tuesday because I (⁸*attend*) _____ an important marketing meeting that day to discuss the new product catalogue.
Sales OK. I (⁹*give*) _____ him the message.
Jeff   That's great. And this bit's really important. (¹⁰*you / make*) _____ sure that you tell Göran that he (¹¹*not /print*) _____ the catalogue until he's spoken to me.
Sales Ah. I think we sent the catalogue off to the printers yesterday. I (¹²*check*) _____ with a colleague. (¹³*you / hold*) _____ the line for a moment, please? ... Hello. I'm afraid it did go out yesterday.
Jeff   Oh no!
Sales (¹⁴*I /call*) _____ the printers and tell them to stop work on the catalogue until further notice?
Jeff   Yes, please. And (¹⁵*you / call*) _____ me back to confirm that they have stopped work on it? It's really important that they don't print it yet.
Sales Sure, no problem. I (¹⁶*get*) _____ back to you in a few minutes.

Vocabulary practice

1 Use the following words to complete the letter below.

whether	unless	however	unfortunately	while	instead of

CROSBY MACHINE PARTS

Cottage Beck Road
Scunthorpe
Nth Lincs
DN14 2GG

Tel 01724 742663
Fax 01724 742666

Mr J Balsham
Super Snacks Ltd
Frodingham Road
Scunthorpe DN17 2JP

Your Ref

Our Ref

10 July 2011

Dear Mr Balsham

Re: Your order of 8 July 2011

Thank you for your order. I am pleased to say that most of the items are in stock and could be dispatched within twenty-four hours.

[1]_____ , the ball bearings (part no. MC-3801X) are temporarily out of stock and could take two to three weeks. [2]_____ , may I suggest that you order the standard MC-3801 bearings [3]_____ the MC-3801X? The MC-3801 would be fine [4]_____ you are planning to run your machine at extremely high capacity.

Could you please let me know [5]_____ you would like to order the standard or upgraded bearings? Would you like us to send the rest of the order [6]_____ you wait for the MC-3801X?

Thank you for your order. I look forward to hearing from you.

Best regards

2 Use the words in the box to complete the sentences from letters below.

delighted	inconvenience	afraid	insist	enclosed
attention	enquiry	regret	contact	grateful

1 We are _delighted_ to hear that the conference was successful.
2 Please find the euro prices _____ as requested.
3 I would be very _____ if you could contact me as soon as possible.
4 I am _____ the items you requested are temporarily out of stock.
5 We apologise for any _____ this may have caused.
6 Please mark the package for the _____ of Ms Vijaya Dhoni.
7 We _____ to inform you that the vacancy has already been filled.
8 Please do not hesitate to _____ us if you have any further enquiries.
9 Thank you for your _____ of 10 November.
10 We _____ that you deal with this very urgent matter at once.

Multi-word verbs 3 **Match the multi-word verbs with the nouns.**

1	put	out		a caller
2	fill	through		a mistake
3	write	up		some information
4	hang	in		a form
5	cross	down		the phone

Confusables 4 **Choose the correct word to complete each sentence.**

1 Please submit a formal *guess / estimate* by 3 September.

2 Could you just leave a quick *note / notice* on my desk?

3 Please accept my *apologises / apologies* for any unnecessary inconvenience.

4 Would it be all right if we *cancelled / postponed* the meeting until next week?

5 You are kindly *required / requested* to settle the account within two weeks.

6 I'll give you my mobile number *in case / unless* I'm out of the office.

7 Alan, could you *remember / remind* me to send that parcel off today?

8 They *denied / refused* to send a replacement part.

Documents 5 **Match the documents with the definitions.**

1	agenda	**a)**	an approximate price quotation
2	invoice	**b)**	a schedule for a meeting
3	article	**c)**	a piece of information on public display
4	estimate	**d)**	a formal message between colleagues
5	note	**e)**	a request for payment
6	guarantee	**f)**	a written promise
7	memo	**g)**	a piece in a newspaper or magazine
8	notice	**h)**	a short informal message

Letter phrases 6 **Match the functions with the extracts.**

apologise   complain   confirm   postpone   recommend   request

1 Could we put it back until after I get back from holiday?

2 Could you please send me your new price list?

3 *You should try ordering them on the internet. It's a lot cheaper.*

4 As discussed, we will be arriving at 10.30 on Monday 16 June.

5 We regret any inconvenience this may cause you.

6 The service to date has been quite unsatisfactory.

Performance

Adjectives

Use   **Adjectives are used in the following ways.**

- before nouns
  *There was a **sharp** rise in earnings.*
- after the verbs *be, become, seem, appear, look, feel, remain*
  *Sales seemed **good** in the third quarter.*

Adverbs

Form   **Adverbs have the following forms.**

*Costs rose **sharply**.*	*(sharp + **ly**)*
*Output increased **steadily**.*	*(steady + **ily**)*
*Share prices fell **dramatically**.*	*(dramatic + **ally**)*
*We update the figures **weekly**.*	*(weekly – **no change**)*

Use   **Adverbs are used in the following ways.**

- after verbs
  *Turnover increased **sharply** during 2010.*
- before adjectives
  *Imports became **increasingly** expensive due to a strong pound.*
- before other adverbs
  *The company did **extremely** well last year.*

Note!   **Some adjectives have irregular adverb forms.**

good – well   fast – fast   late – late   hard – hard

Present perfect

Form   **The present perfect has the following forms.**

I / you / we / they	he / she / it
*Sales **have doubled** since 2006.*	*The company **has grown** quickly.*
*We **haven't made** any profit.*	*She **hasn't seen** the figures yet.*
***Have** they **published** the report yet?*	***Has** he **read** the Annual Report?*

Use   **The present perfect is used in the following ways.**

- to describe actions at an unfinished or indefinite time
  *The company **has made** a lot of changes.*
- to describe situations that started in the past and are still continuing
  (often with *for, since, yet, still, so far, this, in the last*)
  *The company **has been** a plc **since** 2008.*
- to describe changes that affect the present situation (often with *just*)
  *The company **has just increased** its prices by 4.5%.*

Note!   **If the sentence refers to finished time, the past simple must be used.**

*The company ~~has done~~ well last year. (The company **did** well last year.)*

Grammar practice

Adverbs **1 Complete the sentences with the adverb of the adjectives in brackets.**

1 The new product sold (*quick*) ___quickly___ in Brazil.
2 Figures show the company did very (*good*) _____ last year.
3 Over the last three years our shares have risen (*steady*) _____ .
4 The results were published a little (*late*) _____ this year.
5 Our Spanish office submits its sales results (*monthly*) _____ .
6 The company has tried very (*hard*) _____ to reduce its costs.
7 Fuel costs have risen (*dramatic*) _____ this year.
8 We've grown (*fast*) _____ over the last three years.

Adjectives and adverbs **2 Complete the report with the correct form of the words in brackets.**

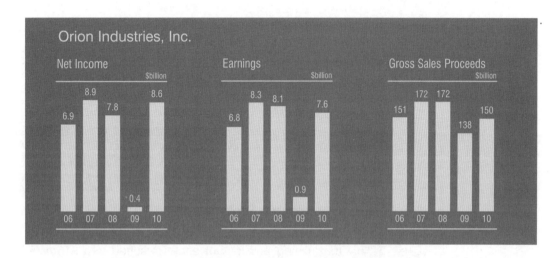

Net income rose (¹*sharp*) ___sharply___ in 2007, before a (²*slight*) _____ fall in 2008. However, there was then a (³*dramatic*) _____ drop to just $0.4bn. In 2010 net income recovered (⁴*strong*) _____ to finish just below 2007 levels at $8.6bn. Earnings also peaked in 2007 before falling (⁵*sudden*) _____ in 2009 to just below $1bn. Earnings made a (⁶*good*) _____ recovery and ended up at $7.6bn in 2010. Gross sales proceeds performed (⁷*good*) _____ in 2007 and remained (⁸*steady*) _____ at $172 the following year before a (⁹*sharp*) _____ drop in 2009. However, in 2010, (¹⁰*strong*) _____ growth saw sales return to the $150bn level.

Present perfect and past simple **3 Complete the dialogue with the correct form of the verbs in brackets.**

Kate   Hello. Kate Hawthorn speaking.
Jason   Hi Kate, it's Jason. I (¹*just / come back*) ___'ve just come back___ from holiday and I was wondering about the quarterly sales figures …
Kate   Oh right. Hang on. We (²*get*) _____ them a couple of weeks ago.
Jason   So, how we (³*we /do*) _____ last quarter?
Kate   Right, here they are. Well, it's difficult to say, really. And I'm afraid some of the offices (⁴*still / not send*) _____ their figures in yet.
Jason   So who (⁵*send*) _____ their results so far?
Kate   Germany. They (⁶*do*) _____ quite well last quarter. They (⁷*beat*) _____ their sales target by 12%.
Jason   How they (⁸*they /manage*) _____ that? Their sales (⁹*be*) _____ down when I (¹⁰*be*) _____ there in August.
Kate   I know, but they (¹¹*win*) _____ a big contract in September.
Jason   So what about Spain?
Kate   We (¹²*not / hear*) _____ from them yet, I'm afraid …

Vocabulary practice

Results **1 Write the words and phrases in the correct groups below.**

> ~~succeed~~   fail   beat   behind   ahead   break even
> overtake   on target   disappointing

positive	neutral	negative
succeed		

2 Use the following words to complete the Chairman's Statement below.

> ~~strategy~~   acquisition   announcement   savings
> expansion   opportunity   recovery   achievement

Cumberland: 2010 Report

Back Forward Reload Home Search Images Print Security Shop Stop

http://www.cumberland.com/financials/2010report/chairman.html

HIGHLIGHTS
FULL FIGURES
CHAIRMAN
REPORT 2009
NOTES
REPORT 2008
REPORT 2007
Press releases
Contact Us
Home

Chairman's Statement 2010

Last year the board promised a [1] _strategy_ that would focus on maximising profits. Our efforts resulted in a $15m reduction in costs. These [2]_____ give us the [3]_____ to invest in the new machinery necessary to further increase our efficiency. We are sure you will agree that this was quite an [4]_____. This new strategy meant we decided not to proceed with the planned $20m [5]_____ of Greystones, a west coast engineering company. Instead, we decided to focus on [6]_____ through increasing sales in our most important markets. This change of focus also produced a [7]_____ of the Cumberland share price on the New York Stock Exchange, which was 40% down on the previous year. The [8]_____ of the withdrawal from the Greystones takeover in the financial press in early March resulted in an immediate 25% rise in the price of Cumberland shares.

Odd one out   **3 Which word is the odd one out?**

1	goal	objective	(sales)	target
2	graph	prediction	chart	diagram
3	profit	expenditure	overheads	costs
4	value	turnover	income	earnings
5	result	forecast	prediction	budget
6	current	present	existing	previous
7	capital	project	finance	assets
8	possibility	chance	position	opportunity

Diagrams **4** **Match the names with the diagrams. Which diagrams could be used to show 1–8?**

> bar chart   pie chart   flow chart   graph

1 sales growth
2 a breakdown of costs
3 a production process
4 profits over several years
5 market share
6 the number of employees
7 share price performance
8 income per product as a %
  of turnover

a)

b)

c)

d)

Cause and effect **5** **Match the sentence halves.**

1 Exports to France decreased due to   a) an increase in market share.
2 A reduction in overheads meant   b) the weakness of the euro.
3 Production times were cut as a result of   c) the $2.2bn acquisition of Indigo.
4 A successful discounting policy led to   d) a sharp fall in the share price.
5 Pre-tax profits were down because of   e) investment in new machinery.
6 Poor third quarter results caused   f) an increase in profitability.

6 **Rewrite the sentences using the correct form of the words in brackets.**

1 It's difficult to export to some countries. They have complex regulations.
  (*due to*)   It's difficult to export to some countries due to complex regulations .
2 We produce locally. The production costs are lower.
  (*because of*) _____ .
3 We're now trading in euros. We've had to update all our systems.
  (*mean*) _____ .
4 There were problems with a supplier so there were delivery delays.
  (*cause*) _____ .
5 Production costs are rising. Margins are getting smaller.
  (*lead to*) _____ .
6 European exports have risen. The value of the euro is falling.
  (*due to*) _____ .
7 It will be easier to distribute directly to customers. Internet usage has increased.
  (*because of*) _____ .
8 There are some new regulations. They will increase our export business.
  (*lead to*) _____ .

Review unit 1 (1–5)

Grammar

1 Complete the sentences with the correct form of the present simple or present continuous.

Sarah   Hi Steve. Are you busy right now?

Steve   Well, I (¹*write*) _____ a report on my trip to Argentina right now. Why?

Sarah   Some visitors (²*arrive*) _____ at the airport in an hour or so and I'm stuck in a meeting …

Steve   And you (³*want*) _____ me to pick them up …

Sarah   Could you? It's just that Mandy (⁴*prepare*) _____ for the sales presentation this afternoon, so she's really busy too.

Steve   OK. What time (⁵*your visitors /arrive*) _____ ?

Sarah   I (⁶*think*) _____ it's something like 9.40 at Tegel. But check with Mandy. She (⁷*have*) _____ all the details of their travel arrangements.

Steve   I (⁸*not /have*) _____ much time.

Sarah   Well, it usually (⁹*take*) _____ about forty minutes to drive to the airport at this time, so you should be OK.

Steve   Who are the visitors?

Sarah   Two salespeople from China. They're here for the presentation.

Steve   (¹⁰*Mandy /know*) _____ their names so I can write them on a board?

Sarah   Just hold up a board with the company name on it. That'll be fine.

Steve   If you say so. Anyway, I'd better go if I'm going to get there in time to meet them.

2 Choose the correct modal verb to complete each sentence.

1 I _____ email you the report this afternoon.
    a) may   **b)** 'll   **c)** must

2 _____ I use your phone, please?
    a) May   **b)** Will   **c)** Should

3 We _____ increase profits to avoid a takeover.
    a) won't   **b)** mustn't   **c)** have to

4 Staff _____ use the internet for personal use.
    a) mustn't   **b)** might not   **c)** needn't

5 We _____ recruit more people until the contract is signed.
    a) would   **b)** shouldn't   **c)** 're allowed to

6 With sales increasing, we _____ now invest in machinery.
    a) can   **b)** would   **c)** don't have to

7 _____ I have a word with you in my office, please?
    a) Shall   **b)** Would   **c)** May

8 We _____ postpone the meeting if you like.
    a) should   **b)** could   **c)** would

9 _____ I help you?
    a) Shall   **b)** Mustn't   **c)** Would

10 _____ you post this for me, please?
    a) Shall   **b)** Must   **c)** Could

3 Complete the sentences with an adjective or an adverb.

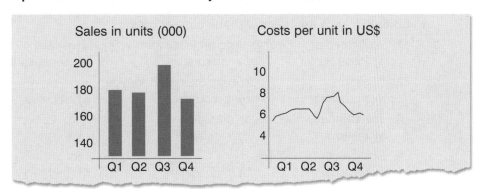

Sales in units (000)

Costs per unit in US$

Sales fell (¹*slight*) ___slightly___ in the second quarter, from 179,000 units to 177,000. Seasonal sales from July–September meant a (²*dramatic*) _____ rise in the third quarter, with sales peaking at 192,000 units. An (³*extreme*) _____ disappointing fourth quarter saw sales fall to 172,000, which was a (⁴*slight*) _____ fall compared to the start of the year. However, compared to last year, annual sales rose (⁵*steady*) _____ to finish 8% up.

In this year's Annual Report, we announced a strategy to cut our unit production costs to below $5 by the end of the year. To begin with, costs rose (⁶*steady*) _____ from $5.5 to $6.3 by the end of May. Cutbacks reduced this figure (⁷*quick*) _____ to $5.6. But the need for extra seasonal workers led to a (⁸*sharp*) _____ rise, which peaked at $8.1 in September, before falling (⁹*steady*) _____ back down to $6.1 per unit by the end of October. Unfortunately, this figure remained (¹⁰*steady*) _____ until the end of the year and we missed our target.

4 Complete the email with the correct form of the past simple or present perfect.

◄ ► **email**   RE: Sales forecasts

From :	George Curtis [curtisgr@sdf.co.uk]
Sent:	Tuesday 19 November 2.17pm
To:	Gemma Hayden
Subject:	**RE: Sales forecasts**

Gemma

Thanks for your email, which I only (¹*get*) ___got___ yesterday. It sounds as if you (²*have*) _____ a great trip to Italy last week. As for the forecasts, I'm afraid they (³*not / all come*) _____ in yet. France and Germany both (⁴*send*) _____ theirs in last week and I (⁵*get*) _____ Spain's this morning. I (⁶*already / ask*) _____ Tessa to send reminders but last year the forecasts (⁷*not / all arrive*) _____ until a week late. (⁸*you / mention*) _____ it to Paolo when you (⁹*be*) _____ in Rome? He (¹⁰*always / be*) _____ very good at sending forecasts.

Anyway, we (¹¹*arrange*) _____ the meeting for Monday and we'll go ahead even if all the forecasts (¹²*not / come*) _____ in. I (¹³*see*) _____ Tom Watkins when I (¹⁴*go*) _____ to Head Office on Friday and he (¹⁵*tell*) _____ me to organise the meeting for Monday. He (¹⁶*just / come*) _____ back from the Frankfurt trade fair and he's full of ideas. I think he (¹⁷*make*) _____ some good contacts there but he (¹⁸*promise*) _____ our sales people they'd all have the new product by May. I bet he (¹⁹*not / tell*) _____ them that we (²⁰*not / even start*) _____ it yet!

Vocabulary

1 Complete each sentence with the correct option.

1 We'll need an _interpreter_ to translate for our Saudi guests.
 a) inspector **b)** interpreter **c)** consultant

2 I'll get my _____ to copy the report for you.
 a) purchaser **b)** accountant **c)** secretary

3 The company now has an annual _____ of $60m.
 a) takeover **b)** estimate **c)** turnover

4 She's recently become a _____ of the trade union.
 a) member **b)** manager **c)** partner

5 Our annual _____ depends on the company's performance that year.
 a) wage **b)** salary **c)** bonus

6 The _____ of the board has called a shareholders' meeting.
 a) consultant **b)** co-ordinator **c)** chairman

7 The _____ industry has been affected by the price of raw materials.
 a) marketing **b)** leisure **c)** manufacturing

8 The company's _____ is in Toulouse so we pay tax to the French government.
 a) headquarters **b)** division **c)** warehouse

9 We're a _____ so we only sell to supermarkets, not consumers.
 a) retailer **b)** chain **c)** wholesaler

10 An official _____ about expenses was circulated on the network.
 a) message **b)** notice **c)** memo

11 We didn't know _____ or not it would sell well in Asian markets.
 a) why **b)** whether **c)** while

12 I had to _____ him to book the hotel rooms in Düsseldorf.
 a) remind **b)** suggest **c)** recommend

13 Just _____ the old prices with a pen, scan it and email it to them.
 a) cancel **b)** draw up **c)** cross out

14 We've already _____ last year's sales figures and it's only September.
 a) risen **b)** beaten **c)** broken even

15 If we're lucky, we won't go over our _____ this year.
 a) balance **b)** figures **c)** budget

16 There's been strong _____ in all our key markets this year.
 a) growth **b)** profit **c)** value

17 The machine _____ burnt out the motor.
 a) operator **b)** assessor **c)** labourer

18 We'll have to ask the shift to do _____ on Saturday.
 a) working hours **b)** business hours **c)** overtime

19 I contribute 5% to my _____ scheme each month.
 a) pension **b)** retirement **c)** unemployment

20 We _____ the company with two friends in 2009.
 a) broke up **b)** drew up **c)** set up

21 Our _____ won't give us the finance we need to expand.
 a) parent company **b)** subsidiary **c)** independent company

22 Since the _____ we've had to change our letterheads and stationery.
 a) monopoly **b)** merger **c)** co-ordination

23 I have to report to the Head of the _____ Department.
 a) Personal **b)** Employee **c)** Personnel

24 We're entering the Latin American market. _____, we're all learning Spanish.
 a) However **b)** Because **c)** Therefore

25 I'm busy. Could you ask her to _____ in about half an hour?
 a) talk back **b)** chat back **c)** call back

26 I'm just calling to _____ the meeting on Monday – the 26th is fine.
   a) postpone   b) update   c) confirm

27 The _____ must be paid in full within thirty days.
   a) note   b) invoice   c) turnover

28 We've been trying to _____ our overheads for the last six months.
   a) fall   b) reduce   c) recover

29 Fast _____ has led to staff shortages in our IT department.
   a) expenditure   b) expansion   c) business

30 We've beaten our sales _____ by about 16% this year.
   a) forecast   b) strategy   c) goal

31 Share prices fell _____ in London due to some panic buying.
   a) steadily   b) sharply   c) slowly

32 There was a _____ in earnings of £52m last year.
   a) launch   b) level   c) fall

33 We _____ about golf for about half an hour on the phone.
   a) chatted   b) discussed   c) talked

34 The takeover was _____ on national television the next day.
   a) acquired   b) announced   c) purchased

35 I circulated the _____ by email in advance of the meeting.
   a) memo   b) agenda   c) guarantee

36 I'm afraid the suggested dates are _____ for Sharon and myself.
   a) disappointing   b) inconvenient   c) urgent

37 We're very _____ for your assistance in this matter.
   a) satisfied   b) delighted   c) grateful

38 They've had a lot of _____ from customers about the poor quality.
   a) complaints   b) recommendations   c) apologies

39 We can't increase sales _____ we lower the price.
   a) whether   b) although   c) unless

40 I've sent the email with the _____ file she wanted.
   a) enclosed   b) attached   c) included

41 Could you please _____ him about the launch dates for the new product?
   a) request   b) demand   c) ask

42 Higher margins meant we made more money even though _____ fell slightly.
   a) profits   b) sales   c) predictions

43 The union _____ has fallen by 50% since 1998.
   a) membership   b) number   c) workforce

44 Unicoat's new production facility is _____ 5km from Glasgow.
   a) located   b) planted   c) settled

45 We've increased our market share faster than our _____, which is good news.
   a) retailers   b) partners   c) rivals

46 The government has done a good job of _____ the economy.
   a) spending   b) co-ordinating   c) running

47 We are sorry for any _____ this may cause you.
   a) regret   b) attention   c) inconvenience

48 We could email it _____ of sending it by post.
   a) in case   b) instead   c) rather

49 ComfyFeet is one of the best selling _____ of shoe in this country.
   a) brands   b) shares   c) promotions

50 We haven't been doing very well in _____ months.
   a) current   b) last   c) recent

Products

Comparatives and superlatives

Form   Adjectives have the following comparative and superlative forms.

	adjective	comparative	superlative
single syllable	*big*	*big**ger***	*the big**gest***
-ly endings	*earl~~y~~*	*earl**ier***	*the earl**iest***
multi-syllable	*expensive*	***more** expensive*	*the **most** expensive*
irregular	*good*	***better***	*the **best***
	bad	***worse***	*the **worst***

Note!   **All comparisons can be made in two ways.**

*Product X **is better than** product Y.*
*Product Y **isn't as good as** product X.*
Product X ~~is better as~~ product Y.

Future arrangements

Form   **Future arrangements can be made in the following ways.**

*We're **launching** the new product in Frankfurt.*
*The show **starts** at 10.30 tomorrow morning.*

Use   **These forms are used in the following ways.**

- to describe events that have been arranged
  *We're **meeting** the researchers tomorrow.*
  *They're **bringing out** a new model next month.*
- to refer to fixed timetables or schedules
  *The plane **leaves** at 10.40.*
  *The dinner **finishes** at 11.00pm.*

Note!   ***Will** is not used to describe future arrangements.*

I ~~will meet~~ Jordi on Friday.
*I'm **meeting** Jordi on Friday.*

Future intentions

Form   **Future intentions can be expressed in the following ways.**

*We're **going to print** the brochures in Egypt.*
*I'**ll send** a price list to you by email.*

Use   **These forms are used in the following ways.**

- to describe existing intentions
  *We're **going to increase** the research budget.*
  *I'm **going to visit** our markets in the USA.*
- to express spontaneous intentions
  *The phone rings: I'**ll get** it.*
  *A customer asks for information: I'**ll send** you a brochure.*

Grammar practice

Comparatives and superlatives

1 **Complete the advertisement with the correct form of the words in brackets.**

PocketPA 2011 – The next generation of smartphone is here

The new PocketPA 2011 is a (¹*light*) _____*lighter*_____ and far (²*powerful*) _____ version of the best-selling PocketPA personal digital organiser.

The new model now has the (³*fast*) _____ chip on the market, allowing it to take full advantage of the (⁴*modern*) _____ technology available today. Now fully 3G-compatible, PocketPA 2011 can surf the internet, making it our (⁵*good*) _____ smartphone to date.

The newly-designed interface is (⁶*easy*) _____ to use than ever before and at just 60 x 105mm it is (⁷*small*) _____ than many of its leading competitors. Priced at £240, the PocketPA 2011 will certainly be one of the (⁸*competitive*) _____ products in the fast growing smartphone market.

Futures

2 **Complete the dialogues with the correct form of the words in brackets.**

1 **A:** When (*you / fly*) ___*are you flying*___ to New York?

   B: I (*leave*) _____ on Wednesday morning.

2 **A:** What time (*the plane /land*) _____ ?

   B: It (*land*) _____ at 2.50 in the morning.

3 **A:** Where (*we /meet*) _____ this afternoon?

   B: In the boardroom, I think.

   A: There's already a meeting in there this afternoon.

   B: Oh, OK. Then we (*meet*) _____ in Mina's office.

4 **A:** I'm afraid Mr Jacobson isn't available at the moment. Can I take a message?

   B: No, it's OK, I (*send*) _____ him an email.

5 **A:** Have you thought about the colour of the new jackets?

   B: Yes, we have. They (*be*) _____ blue.

6 **A:** Have you seen the itinerary for the press launch?

   B: No, I haven't. When (*the press /arrive*) _____ ?

7 **A:** Hurry up! The plane (*leave*) _____ in half an hour.

   B: OK. OK. I (*just / call*) _____ the office.

8 **A:** I think some of our products are looking a bit old now.

   B: I know. We (*update*) _____ the range. We're just not sure when.

9 **A:** What (*you /call*) _____ the new product?

   B: No idea. We (*do*) _____ some market research next month.

10 **A:** Our competitors (*bring out*) _____ a new product in June.

   B: I know. That's why we (*bring forward*) _____ the launch of our own new product by three weeks.

Vocabulary practice

1 Use the clues below to find eighteen adjectives in the puzzle describing products.

A	D	V	A	N	C	E	D	A	U	E	T
D	E	C	O	N	O	M	I	C	A	L	H
C	F	D	T	N	D	I	F	G	F	W	I
R	E	L	I	A	B	L	E	H	L	P	N
S	C	B	N	G	S	U	P	T	E	O	M
H	T	O	Y	C	H	E	A	P	X	P	O
O	I	R	M	R	P	O	Y	I	I	U	D
R	V	I	O	P	O	R	T	A	B	L	E
T	E	N	D	N	A	T	O	V	L	A	R
H	U	G	E	W	G	C	A	B	E	R	N
O	U	T	O	F	D	A	T	E	O	D	T
P	O	E	X	P	E	N	S	I	V	E	G

Describe a product that …

1 ~~has the latest technology~~
2 does not work properly
3 fits a lot into a small space
4 is old-fashioned
5 does not cost a lot
6 is uninteresting
7 is very big
8 never breaks down
9 can be carried anywhere
10 is not weak
11 is very small
12 costs a lot
13 is used by a lot of people
14 is not very thick
15 can be used in different ways
16 is not very long
17 is not old
18 is cheap to run

2 Complete the table.

adjective	opposite	noun
accurate	inaccurate	_____
available	_____	_____
_____	incapable	_____
_____	_____	flexibility
comfortable	_____	_____
_____	inconvenient	_____
efficient	_____	_____
_____	_____	popularity

Product warranties

3 Use the following words to complete the warranty below.

guarantee	replacement	consumer	customer service
return	condition	wear and tear	non-standard

Under the terms of this ¹_____, the customer has the right to ²_____ any product that is defective or in a poor ³_____. This does not apply to any product that has suffered natural ⁴_____ or has been damaged through negligence or fitted with ⁵_____ parts as the result of a customer installation.

All damaged or faulty goods should be sent to the ⁶_____ department and you will be issued with a ⁷_____ product of the same type. This will not affect your ⁸_____ rights.

Dimensions

4 Complete the table.

adjective	noun	measurement
high	_height_	centimetres / metres
long	_____	centimetres / metres
_____	width	_____
deep	_____	centimetres / metres
fast	_____	kilometres per hour
_____	_____	kilogrammes

Describing products

5 Match the opposite adjectives. Then use one of each pair to complete the sentences.

positive	negative
huge	heavy
brand new	tiny
exciting	weak
reliable	ugly
attractive	out of date
strong	expensive
economical	boring
portable	defective

1 Compared to the huge old version, this one's ____tiny____ .
2 The S2000 is _____ so you can carry it with you wherever you go.
3 Its design had become _____ so we had to stop making it.
4 Low fuel consumption makes it one of the most _____ cars on the road.
5 We had to withdraw the new product due to a _____ component.
6 Customers found the design sample _____ and lacking any real interest.
7 Most people thought it looked ugly but some found it very _____ .
8 Its ultra-hard plastic casing means it's very _____ .

Office equipment

Imperatives

Form   **Positive forms use the infinitive.**

Press 'delete' to remove the file.

Negative forms use Don't or Never.

Don't / Never leave the photocopier on overnight.

Use   **Imperatives are used in the following ways.**

* to give orders or instructions
  Call the engineer if it doesn't work.
* to make informal requests (often made more polite with *will you?*)
  Pass me that pen, will you?

Countable and uncountable nouns

Form   **Countable and uncountable nouns have the following forms.**

countable	uncountable
a computer	*an equipment*
two computers	*two equipments*
	Uncountable nouns take a singular verb.

Use   **Countable and uncountable nouns are used in the following ways.**

There is a printer.   *There is some equipment.*
There are some memory sticks.
There are a lot of books.   *There is a lot of paper.*
There aren't many staples.   *There isn't much toner.*
We only have a few computers.   *There is a little stationery left.*

Some and any

Use   **Some and any are used in the following ways.**

* *Some* refers to an unspecified quantity.
  We've got some new computers.
  I don't like some of their products.
* *Any* refers to a complete lack of something.
  There isn't any coffee left.
* *Any* is used to form questions. (*Some* is also used in polite requests.)
  Do you have any paper for the printer?
  Would you like some coffee?

Note!   **Negatives with there is / are can be formed in two ways.**

There isn't any paper left.   *There aren't any chairs left.*
There's no paper left.   *There are no chairs left.*

Grammar practice

Imperatives

1 Use the correct form of the following verbs to complete the instructions below.

~~install~~ delete dial file phone tick email stop

1 _Don't install_ the new software until you have removed the old version first.
2 To get an outside line, _____ nine first and then the number.
3 _____ the document to her – the network is down.
4 Make a copy of the invoice and _____ it in the payments folder.
5 _____ the video until they've seen the bit about our new products.
6 Look at the list and _____ the ones you want.
7 _____ him now – he's in a meeting and doesn't want to be disturbed.
8 _____ the old files. Copy them onto a USB memory stick and keep it safe.

Countable and uncountable nouns

2 Write the words in the correct groups below.

~~DVD~~ information catalogue email stationery program support equipment hardware money price diary network news stock

countable nouns	uncountable nouns
DVD	

3 Find and correct the mistake in each line of the text.

> **To:** All staff
> **Re:** Ordering office equipment
>
> 1 Please note that all <u>equipments</u> must be ordered through   _equipment_
> 2 Joanne. Recently, much orders have been placed separately by   _____
> 3 different members of staff, causing many confusion. All orders   _____
> 4 must be on proper order forms – if there aren't much of these   _____
> 5 left, inform Joanne so she can print out any more. Recently,   _____
> 6 we've had a little delays with deliveries of paper, so please order   _____
> 7 all stationeries in good time. Orders take about a week to arrive.   _____
> 8 Could staff please show a few understanding and give Joanne   _____
> 9 catalogue numbers – she has a work of her own to do and   _____
> 10 doesn't want to waste some time looking through office supply   _____
> catalogues finding this information for you.

Vocabulary practice

1 Use the clues below to find sixteen items from the office in the puzzle.

S	T	A	S	C	L	D	E	R	N	O	P
P	S	S	T	A	T	I	O	N	E	R	Y
H	P	C	A	L	C	U	L	A	T	O	R
O	R	I	M	E	O	D	N	E	W	A	A
T	I	S	P	N	D	O	I	E	O	S	I
O	N	S	E	D	I	E	P	S	R	F	D
C	T	O	F	A	X	O	S	P	K	O	S
O	E	R	T	R	L	F	R	K	A	L	F
P	R	S	K	E	Y	B	O	A	R	D	G
I	T	I	V	Y	P	S	W	T	O	E	H
E	O	N	O	S	T	A	P	L	E	R	O
R	E	R	U	L	E	R	D	I	P	U	P

Find something you use to …

1 ~~post letters in~~
2 help you work out figures
3 plan the year ahead
4 put your computer on
5 keep appointments in
6 organise loose sheets of paper
7 connect several computers
8 type with

9 duplicate documents
10 output from a computer
11 put on an envelope before posting
12 cut paper or string
13 measure length
14 attach sheets of paper
15 write letters on
16 take notes on

2 Match the nouns. Then use them to complete the sentences below.

DVD   stamp
word   player
filing   list
air-   clip
memory   processor
paper   cabinet
rubber   conditioning
price   stick

1 I'll need a _DVD player_ to show the trainees the health and safety film.
2 Our office is always cold because of the _____ system.
3 I've only got an old computer because I only ever use it as a _____ .
4 Make sure the _____ includes the euro conversions, won't you?
5 I've run out of staples so you'll have to use a _____ to attach it.
6 I think they're in the _____ under Invoices Paid 2010.
7 I can't get an internet connection here, so I'll copy the data on to a _____ .
8 Make sure you mark the invoice as paid. There's a _____ on my desk.

Office supplies **3** **Match the verbs with the nouns then complete the sentences below.**

try out		faulty machine
fill in		new software
print out	a / an	computer
switch off	the	toner
run out of	some	paper tray
take away		order form
fill up		report

1 We'll _try out some new software_ to see if it runs OK on the network.
2 _____ when you leave, won't you? It was left on last night.
3 People never _____ when the photocopier runs out of paper!
4 I have to _____ today but my computer keeps crashing.
5 Make sure you write in capital letters when you _____ .
6 The copier's _____ again. Do we have another cartridge?
7 If our engineer can't fix it on site, he'll _____ .

4 **Complete the word diagram with the following office items.**

~~instructions~~   out of order   memory   form   defective
quotation   hardware   guarantee   invoice   receipt   faulty
cable   program   service agreement   out of stock

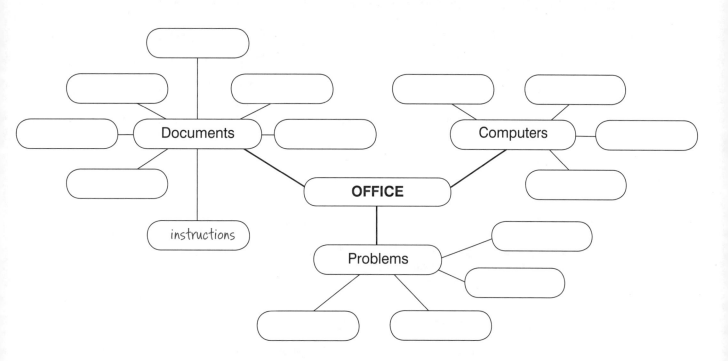

Confusables **5** **Choose the correct word to complete each sentence.**

1 I guess this socket here is where the monitor *cable / wire* plugs in.
2 It's cold here. Can we turn up the *air-conditioning / central heating*?
3 We get all our equipment from a local office *supplier / purchaser*.
4 It doesn't work. I'm afraid it's out of *stock / order*.
5 The light's gone again. We'll have to change the *bulb / lamp*.
6 I think there are 250 *sheets / pages* of paper in each pack.

Business travel

Infinitives

Form   Infinitives are usually used with *to*. However, modal verbs are never followed by *to*.

*We **arranged to meet** in Poznan in May.*
*I **couldn't find** a cheap flight to Turin.*

Negative forms use *not* + infinitive.

*She **chose not to stay** at the Plaza Hotel.*

Use   Infinitives are used in the following ways.

- after certain verbs (see the list below)
  *I **managed to get** a room at the last minute.*
- after certain verbs + an object
  *She **asked me to get** some foreign currency for her.*
- after adjectives (often with *too* or *enough*)
  *It's **important to have** a high-speed internet connection in your room.*

Note!   **These verbs are often followed by an infinitive.**

verbs without an object

			verbs with an object
afford	decide	offer	ask
agree	demand	plan	expect
aim	hope	prepare	invite
appear	intend	promise	remind
arrange	manage	refuse	tell
choose	need	want	warn

Predictions

Form   **Predictions can be made in the following ways.**

*Moscow **is going to become** colder next week.*
*It**'ll be** too late to get a hotel soon.*
*The poor results **are likely to continue**. (also bound to, set to, unlikely to)*

Use   **These forms are used in the following ways.**

- for spoken predictions based on knowledge / evidence
  *We**'re going to be** late if we don't hurry up.*
- for spontaneous spoken predictions
  *Another delay? This means we**'ll miss** our connecting flight.*
- for written predictions in newspapers / magazines
  *The hotel sector **will continue** to grow over the next ten years.*
  *The company **is set to recruit** 1,500 new workers.*

Note!   **Other modal verbs can also be used to make predictions.**

*There **could be** some delays at the airport.*
*We **might not leave** until Saturday afternoon.*

Grammar practice

Infinitives **1** **Match the sentence halves.**

1 After such a bad year we can't afford   a) not to tell anyone.
2 The project planning program makes it easy   b) to take on new staff.
3 The new project's a secret so I told her   c) to stay there again.
4 I didn't have cash and the receptionist refused   d) to produce travel schedules.
5 The hotel was dirty. They can't expect us   e) to accept my credit card.
6 The food was cold so the manager agreed   f) not to charge us for it.
7 Money's short right now so it's important   g) to meet next week.
8 We spoke yesterday and arranged   h) to reduce our travel expenses.

2 **Use the following verbs to report the speakers' words below.**

> ~~invite~~   ask   remind   refuse   promise   warn

1 'If you come to Turin, you really must visit our offices.'
  She invited me to visit their offices in Turin.

2 'I definitely won't book that hotel again.'
  _____

3 'Don't forget to take the new brochures with you.'
  _____

4 'Whatever you do, don't go into the east part of the city at night.'
  _____

5 'I'm sorry, but I just haven't got the time to do the report.'
  _____

6 'Could you please not take next week off?'
  _____

Predictions **3** **Write predictions with *going to* based on the newspaper headlines.**

1 EBA to cut 400 jobs

2 AirEast to launch Executive Class

3 Shanghai hotel prices set to rise

4 Stansted airport announces new expansion plans
By Vikram Patel

5 Euro unlikely to recover against US dollar in near future

6 Strike will hit London underground says union

1 _I see EBA's going to cut 400 jobs._
2 _____
3 _____
4 _____
5 _____
6 _____

Vocabulary practice

Air travel **1** **Match the nouns. Then use them to complete the text below.**

terminal	card
passport	building
check-in	officer
departure	baggage
duty-free	shops
excess	control
boarding	desk
customs	board
information	lounge

Make sure you know which ¹ _terminal building_ you need before you arrive at the airport. Then proceed to the ² _____ , where the reservations agent will look at your ticket and weigh your luggage to see if there is any ³ _____ to pay. Once you have checked in, you are given a ⁴ _____ and asked to go to the ⁵ _____ . To get there, you have to go through security, which means showing your documents at ⁶ _____ and then having your luggage checked by a ⁷ _____ . Once through security, you have to wait for your flight to be called. You can also look around the ⁸ _____ and perhaps buy souvenirs. But you must remember to keep an eye on the ⁹ _____ for your flight announcement.

Food **2** **Complete the word diagram with the following items of food.**

beef   onion   orange   peas   turkey   potato   pork   pepper
pear   corn   cod   lamb   bacon   lettuce   strawberry   mushroom
carrot   plaice   sausage   chicken   spinach   celery   cauliflower

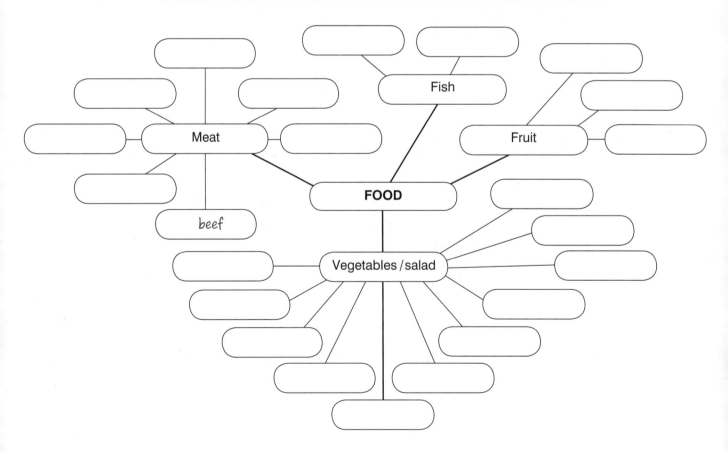

Booking a hotel **3** **Use the following words and phrases to complete the dialogue below.**

reservation	breakfast	parking	balcony	check out
fortnight	mini-bar	plug in	bill	non-smoking

Hotel   Hello. The Park Plaza.
Caller   Hello, I'd like to make a ¹_____ , please.
Hotel   Certainly, Sir. For how many nights?
Caller   A ²_____ , please. Starting from Saturday 12 May.
Hotel   So, that's fourteen nights from 12 May. Would you like a ³_____ room?
Caller   Yes, please. And a room with a ⁴_____ , if possible. The views over the
          river should be great at this time of year.
Hotel   They are. Would you like ⁵_____ included?
Caller   No, it's OK. I'll get something in a café. Oh, do you have ⁶_____
          facilities at the hotel?
Hotel   We do, Sir. Behind the hotel. I can reserve you a space if you like.
Caller   That'd be great. Thanks.
Hotel   Anything else?
Caller   Yes, do your rooms have ethernet sockets? I need to ⁷_____ my
          computer so I can send reports back to the office while I'm there.
Hotel   That's no problem. All our rooms have Wi-Fi, satellite television, a
          ⁸_____ and air-conditioning.
Caller   Oh good. One last thing. Could you send the ⁹_____ directly to my
          company, rather than me paying it myself?
Hotel   Sure. Just leave a business card with reception when you ¹⁰_____ .
          Could I have the name you want on the invoice, please?
Caller   My name's Patrick Stone but the company's called FX Communications.
Hotel   So that's fourteen nights from 12 May under the name FX Communications?
Caller   That's right.
Hotel   OK, Mr Stone. We'll see you on the 12th. Thank you for calling. Goodbye.
Caller   Thanks. Bye.

Multi-word verbs **4** **Match the multi-word verbs with the noun phrases.**

1 set   in   on a journey
2 plug   off   at the airport
3 check   out   a jacket
4 take   on   a computer
5 get   off   of a hotel
6 check   in   a plane

Confusables **5** **Choose the correct word to complete each sentence.**

1 Men are expected to wear a *shirt*/*skirt* and tie in the office.
2 I managed to get all my clothes into just one *briefcase*/*suitcase* this time.
3 Claudia looked very elegant in her jacket and *trousers*/*tights*.
4 All male guests have to wear a *tie*/*collar* at the gala dinner.
5 It was really hot but we had to keep our *raincoats*/*jackets* on in the meeting.
6 I was invited to a colleague's house and had to take my *shoes*/*socks* off.
7 At this time of year, Pietro, I think you should take a light *blouse*/*jacket* with you.
8 She looked really good at the presentation. She wore a dark blue *suit*/*costume*.
9 You'll need *overalls*/*an overcoat* if you're going there at this time of year.

Conferences

Time clauses

Form When referring to future time, *before, after, when, as soon as* and *until* are followed by present simple verbs.

*We're going to wait here **until** the conference **starts**.*
*We'll go to lunch **as soon as** she **gets** here.*

Note! We can use the present perfect to emphasise that one action is complete before another one starts.

*We can continue the meeting **after** we've **finished** lunch.*

Indefinite article (*a /an*)

Use *A / an* is used in the following ways.

- to refer to general singular countable nouns
  *There's **a presentation** on leadership at 2 o'clock this afternoon.*
  *We'll have **an hour** for lunch.*
- to refer to jobs
  *I'm **an accountant**.*

Definite article (*the*)

Use The definite article is used in the following ways.

- to refer to nouns already mentioned
  *We can go by taxi or subway. **The taxi** will be quicker.*
- to refer to nouns that are defined
  *That's **the conference centre I told you about**.*
- to refer to nouns that are unique
  *The conference centre was on the banks of **the River Seine**.*
- to refer to superlatives
  *It's **the best** conference I've ever been to.*
- to refer to countries with *republic, kingdom, states* etc. in their name.
  *Last year's sales conference was in **the Czech Republic**.*

Zero article (Ø)

Use No article is used in the following situations.

- to refer to general uncountable or general plural nouns
  *We need **(Ø) information** on prices.*
  *I'm trying to find out about **(Ø) facilities**.*
- to refer to proper names
  *I work for **(Ø) Siemens** in **(Ø) Hong Kong**.*
  *She's in **(Ø) Finance**.*

Note! Proper names include the names of

departments   companies   sectors   cities   countries

Grammar practice

Time clauses   **1 Match the sentence halves.**

1 We can't allocate the room numbers   **a)** until everyone's arrived.

2 Don't forget to lower the lights   **b)** until everyone checks in.

3 You'll be asked to present your ideas   **c)** after you finish the workshops.

4 I'll email you the agenda   **d)** before the main speaker starts.

5 We'll wait in the lobby   **e)** as soon as I've prepared it.

6 We've got time to plan the next session   **f)** when we have lunch.

2 Complete the sentences with the correct form of the verbs in brackets.

1 We (*leave*) ___*'ll leave*___ for the restaurant when the coach (*arrive*) ___*arrives*___ in about ten minutes.

2 We (*serve*) _____ coffee when people (*finish*) _____ their lunches.

3 After all the regional sales managers (*make*) _____ their presentations, we (*have*) _____ a quick break for about twenty minutes.

4 Sarah (*book*) _____ the venue as soon as she (*receive*) _____ some information about the number of delegates.

5 I (*check*) _____ the projector before I (*start*) _____ my session.

6 Until we (*know*) _____ the final numbers, we (*not / book*) _____ any hotel rooms.

7 I'm afraid I (*have to*) _____ leave before the final session (*start*) _____ .

8 After we (*finish*) _____ dinner, there (*be*) _____ a short prize-giving.

Articles   **3 Complete the email with *a, an, the* or the zero article (Ø).**

◄ ►   **email**   **RE: Wroclaw conference**

From :	Glass, Susan [sjglass@interform.com]
Sent:	Wednesday 1 August 2.17pm
To:	Xiang, LiMei
Subject:	RE: Hong Kong conference

Li Mei

Thanks for [1]___*the*___ email yesterday. It sounds as if you're really getting [2]___Ø___ things organised for [3]_____ conference in [4]_____ Hong Kong. Have you finalised [5]_____ agenda yet? It's just that Jing – the new girl in [6]_____ Marketing – wants to do [7]_____ session on her research project. She's been working on it all summer, so it would be great if you could find [8]_____ place for her on [9]_____ agenda.

I hope you've found [10]_____ nice restaurant for [11]_____ welcome dinner. Do you remember that restaurant we went to in [12]_____ Kuala Lumpur last year? Even [13]_____ Chairman had a bit too much wine that night! I think [14]_____ Malaysia conference was [15]_____ best annual sales conference I've been to so far, so that's what you've got to beat!

All the best
Susan

Vocabulary practice

Agendas **1** **Use the following words to complete the conference agenda below.**

~~breakfast~~ sandwiches speech launch delegates refreshments
show stand presentation seminar break tea

IDD 2011 Conference, Hong Kong

Saturday 20 February

07.30   ¹ _Breakfast_ in the garden restaurant – choice of traditional cooked and continental style

09.00   Opening ²_____ by CEO Joshua Moore

09.15   ³_____ of regional sales figures for 2011 (Room 100)

10.30   Coffee ⁴_____ – in the Sunset lounge

11.00   Effective Sales Forecasting ⁵_____ (Room 100)

12.30   Buffet lunch with ⁶_____ and other light ⁷_____ . Served in the 'Harbour Restaurant' (first floor)

14.00   New Product ⁸_____ including sound and light ⁹_____ (Main Conference Hall)

15.30   Afternoon ¹⁰_____ – served in the Sunset lounge

16.00   'Objective 2012'

         All ¹¹_____ are recommended to visit the company ¹²_____ in the hotel lobby to meet local staff

Word formation **2** **Complete the table. Then use the correct form of the words to complete the sentences.**

person	verb	noun
participant	participate	_participation_
_____	speak	
_____	_____	specialisation
attendee		_____
promoter	promote	_____
presenter	_____	_____
_____	_____	guide
host/ess	_____	hosting

1   There was a lot of delegate _participation_ – especially in the workshops.
2   The seminar will be of particular interest to IT _____ .
3   The catering team did a great job of _____ the visitors.
4   One workshop was very poorly _____ with only six people there.
5   I think our _____ did a great job of advertising the product launch.
6   The CEO gave a very short and humorous _____ to open the conference.
7   Bob's generally a good speaker but this _____ wasn't very interesting.
8   Lin Yao was our _____ . She showed us around all the city's sights.

Arranging a conference

3 Use the following words and phrases to complete the dialogue below.

> attend   crowded   venue   bring forward   trade fair
> advance booking   rearrange   invitations

Jing   Hello, Marketing.
Chris   Jing, it's Chris.
Jing   Hi Chris. How are you doing?
Chris   Good, thanks. Listen, I need to talk to you about next year's training weekend.
Jing   What about it?
Chris   Well, Jia Li says it's on the 24–26 June, which is the same weekend as the Tokyo
^{1}_____ .
Jing   Is that a problem?
Chris   Well, all our trainees will have to ^{2}_____ it, so they won't be here. Could you ^{3}_____ the dates by a couple of weeks?
Jing   It's not that easy to just ^{4} _____ it all, you know, Chris. We've already made an ^{5}_____ and I don't know whether the ^{6}_____ will charge a cancellation fee.
Chris   We'd be giving them plenty of notice …
Jing   And I've already printed out all the ^{7}_____ .
Chris   But you haven't sent them yet, have you?
Jing   Which weekend did you have in mind?
Chris   How about the 10–12 June? Two weeks earlier.
Jing   There's the International Technology Exhibition in the city that weekend. All the hotels will be ^{8}_____ and we'll have problems getting rooms.
Chris   OK. How about the 3–5 June?
Jing   It should be OK. I'll try the conference centre but I'm not paying a cancellation fee, Chris. If they ask for one, I'm leaving the booking as it is. OK?
Chris   All right. See what you can do Jing. Thanks.
Jing   I'll get back to you later this week.

Facilities

4 Match the complaints with the hotel facilities.

> lift   shower   bathroom   dry-cleaning   buffet lunch   dining room

1   *"It was a real disappointment – nothing more than a small snack really. I was hungry all afternoon in the sales presentations."*

2   *"It was so annoying – I just couldn't get it right. It would be freezing one moment so I'd turn the tap and then it was too hot."*

3   *"It didn't work all weekend. I must have walked up thousands of steps!"*

4   *"It was really small and the service was pretty slow too. But the worst thing was the cigarette smoke. I went to a restaurant the next night."*

5   *"It was dirty and I don't think they changed the towels during my stay."*

6   *"I thought it'd be a good idea to get my suit freshened up but the so-called 24-hour service took two days and I ended up having to borrow a suit for my presentation. It didn't even fit properly. What a disaster it was!"*

Review unit 2 (7–11)

Grammar

1 **Complete the sentences with the correct future form.**

1 They (*fly*) _____ to Shanghai on 23 June.

2 We can go to the restaurant when the bus (*arrive*) _____ .

3 What time (*the guests /arrive*) _____ tomorrow?

4 We (*need*) _____ to order more stationery soon.

5 I can email it before I (*leave*) _____ for the airport.

6 Sorry Tina, someone's waiting for me. I (*call*) _____ you back.

7 They (*not /manage*) _____ to launch the new product on time.

8 We can break for coffee after the workshops (*finish*) _____ .

9 The plans have changed. We (*not /go*) _____ to Stuttgart now.

10 John needs new brochures so I (*send*) _____ him some today.

2 **Choose the correct option to complete the note.**

Zhi

I'm out of the office for ¹_____ days, so could you order the following supplies this week?

- We don't have ²_____ A4 paper left. I think there are ³_____ boxes in the cupboard. But could you order ⁴_____ more?
- Also, there aren't ⁵_____ highlighters left – what's happened to them all? There are never ⁶_____ left when I look in the cupboard! Anyway, order ⁷_____ more and keep ⁸_____ in your desk for safe-keeping.
- I don't know how ⁹_____ envelopes we have left. Check and order ¹⁰_____ more if we need them.
- Oh, I nearly forgot – there's only ¹¹_____ coffee left in the kitchen. Could you get ¹²_____ more and check the teabag situation. If there are only ¹³_____ left, order more.

There should be ¹⁴_____ money in the petty cash. If there isn't ¹⁵_____ , use my company credit card.

1	**a)** a few	**b)** some	**c)** a little
2	**a)** some	**b)** any	**c)** many
3	**a)** a little	**b)** a few	**c)** many
4	**a)** any	**b)** many	**c)** some
5	**a)** a few	**b)** many	**c)** much
6	**a)** some	**b)** a few	**c)** any
7	**a)** much	**b)** any	**c)** some
8	**a)** a few	**b)** a little	**c)** many
9	**a)** few	**b)** much	**c)** many
10	**a)** many	**b)** much	**c)** a few

11	**a)** a few	**b)** a little	**c)** not much
12	**a)** some	**b)** any	**c)** little
13	**a)** a little	**b)** a few	**c)** many
14	**a)** many	**b)** much	**c)** a little
15	**a)** a little	**b)** any	**c)** many

3 Complete the sentences with the correct comparative or superlative form.

1 Have you seen Jane's new monitor? It's a lot (*big*) _bigger than_ the ones we're using. I hope this means we're all going to get the same.

2 In terms of development costs, it's (*expensive*) _____ product we've ever brought to market. It has to sell well or we're going to lose a lot of money.

3 Sales have been absolutely terrible this year. In fact, I think it's probably been one of (*bad*) _____ I can ever remember.

4 The new receptionist is much (*friendly*) _____ the old one.

5 Nowadays flying is (*cheap*) _____ taking the train in the UK.

6 The new model is far (*economical*) _____ the old S20.

7 I know it looks great. But I think you'll find it isn't as (*fast*) _____ the system we're already using.

8 It looks as if Friday is (*convenient*) _____ day of the week for me, so should we pencil in a meeting at about two or two thirty?

9 Just when you think it can't get any (*bad*) _____ , your computer crashes!

10 The new photocopier's arrived. It can do the same as the old one but it isn't (*large*) _____ . So, there'll be a lot more space in the stationery room.

4 Complete the email with *a, an, the* or Ø (no article).

◀ ▶ ⌂ email	RE: New brochures

From :	Sharon Collins [sjcollins@enitech-esa.com]
Sent:	Wednesday 7 March 10.03am
To:	John Burgess
Subject:	RE: New brochures

John

I've sent ¹____ new sales brochure out to most of the markets now. I sent a thousand out to ²____ USA and five hundred to each of ³____ European offices. ⁴____ US brochures had dollar price lists and ⁵____ European ones had all their prices shown in ⁶____ euros. All price lists went by email as ⁷____ attachment. So they're all right up to date and our offices can also make ⁸____ changes as they wish.

⁹____ US brochures should get there on Thursday – hopefully in time for ¹⁰____ Dallas Trade Fair. Dale Hemmings thinks there might be ¹¹____ problem with US customers not liking multilingual brochures. I explained to him that it was ¹²____ economic decision, as producing five separate monolingual brochures would add too much to ¹³____ marketing budget. He asked whether, in future, they could produce ¹⁴____ brochure of their own for US distribution. Do you think that would that be ¹⁵____ good idea?

Vocabulary

Complete each sentence with the correct option.

1 It's very fuel _efficient_ so it should save customers money.
   a) efficient   **b)** attractive   **c)** flexible

2 I like the _____ but the content of the brochure worries me.
   a) sample   **b)** design   **c)** comfort

3 It's completely _____ so customers will be able to use it anywhere.
   a) light   **b)** portable   **c)** compact

4 The paint began to _____ after just two weeks' use so we sent it back.
   a) fall off   **b)** run out   **c)** hang up

5 Make sure we get three _____ to compare prices before we buy one.
   a) quotations   **b)** orders   **c)** purchases

6 It's about 240cm _____ from side to side.
   a) deep   **b)** high   **c)** wide

7 Make sure it's turned off before you _____ the power on.
   a) switch   **b)** push   **c)** dial

8 The power _____ should be plugged into the special floor sockets.
   a) lines   **b)** wires   **c)** cables

9 I'm sorry but they're out of _____ . We should have some next week.
   a) date   **b)** stock   **c)** order

10 Just _____ the order form and email it to the supplier.
   a) fill in   **b)** file   **c)** fold

11 Go through the file and _____ anything that's now incorrect.
   a) duplicate   **b)** display   **c)** delete

12 I'll send an email to everyone on the _____ .
   a) network   **b)** computers   **c)** program

13 I think the parts are covered for a year but I'll look on the _____ and check.
   a) receipt   **b)** invoice   **c)** guarantee

14 I've nothing to check in. I've just got my _____ here with some papers in it.
   a) suitcase   **b)** baggage   **c)** briefcase

15 I don't like flying. I get really nervous when the plane _____ .
   a) starts   **b)** takes off   **c)** departs

16 Carrying the brochures meant I had to pay _____ baggage at the check in.
   a) extra   **b)** over   **c)** excess

17 I usually like meat but I don't really like _____ for some reason.
   a) turkey   **b)** pear   **c)** onion

18 Michael always wears a _____ and tie when he travels on business.
   a) skirt   **b)** blouse   **c)** shirt

19 I need a room with a broadband socket to _____ my laptop into.
   a) attach   **b)** plug   **c)** connect

20 We had a really good _____ here. It went very quickly.
   a) fly   **b)** plane   **c)** flight

21 You get your _____ from the check-in desk when you arrive at the airport.
   a) ticket   **b)** boarding card   **c)** visa

22 There were about 150 _____ at this year's conference.
   a) delegates   **b)** invitations   **c)** hosts

23 I'm very _____ . I haven't eaten anything all day.
   a) thirsty   **b)** empty   **c)** hungry

24 The press _____ was held at a top Singapore hotel.
   a) marketing   **b)** promotion   **c)** launch

25 We had a _____-style lunch with sandwiches and lots of other things.
   a) buffet   **b)** refreshments   **c)** snack

26 The Asia conference is held at the same _____ every year.
    a) stand   **b)** venue   **c)** booking

27 Our new Quick-meals are very _____ and easy to prepare.
    a) available   **b)** reliable   **c)** convenient

28 The speeches were long and _____ , not very interesting at all really.
    a) accurate   **b)** boring   **c)** capable

29 The new model's very _____ so it should reduce our returns and complaints.
    a) reliable   **b)** popular   **c)** efficient

30 We should have taken note of the copier's _____ , especially the width.
    a) functions   **b)** measurements   **c)** components

31 I need to post a letter. Have you got a _____ for me?
    a) stamp   **b)** staple   **c)** disk

32 They're going to _____ some new software on my computer tomorrow.
    a) delete   **b)** file   **c)** install

33 Order some more A4 paper from the office _____ department, will you?
    a) supplies   **b)** support   **c)** ordering

34 I'm looking for an A4 _____ to send this letter in.
    a) folder   **b)** envelope   **c)** file

35 If you're having problems with your computer, phone the _____ department.
    a) PC   **b)** IT   **c)** CD

36 This computer's very slow because it's old and it hasn't got much _____ .
    a) hardware   **b)** technology   **c)** memory

37 I'm sorry but that product is temporarily _____ .
    a) unsuccessful   **b)** unavailable   **c)** unexciting

38 I think _____ is one of my favourite kinds of fish.
    a) cod   **b)** lamb   **c)** corn

39 Pay for the meal at the hotel _____ when you check out in the morning.
    a) reservations   **b)** reception   **c)** restaurant

40 The light's gone on my desk – I think the _____ needs replacing.
    a) lamp   **b)** bulb   **c)** socket

41 Hang on. I'll quickly make a note of that date in my _____ .
    a) calendar   **b)** diary   **c)** agenda

42 Thank you very much for the _____ to speak at your conference.
    a) invitation   **b)** introduction   **c)** instruction

43 If you want to order some paper, you'll have to _____ an order form.
    a) fill up   **b)** fill in   **c)** try out

44 The chairman gave an excellent opening _____ .
    a) show   **b)** chat   **c)** speech

45 I think _____ are my favourite kind of fruit.
    a) peppers   **b)** peas   **c)** strawberries

46 We've had quality problems with the T100 and a high number of _____ .
    a) returns   **b)** replies   **c)** responses

47 I spent the whole trade fair on our _____ .
    a) stand   **b)** show   **c)** display

48 Do you mind if I bring the meeting _____ a few days?
    a) ahead   **b)** up   **c)** forward

49 I managed to send some emails from the departure _____ at the airport.
    a) lounge   **b)** terminal   **c)** area

50 I take several pairs of _____ if I'm going to be wearing skirts.
    a) trousers   **b)** overalls   **c)** tights

Processes

Passive

Form   **The passive has the following form.**

subject + correct tense of the verb *be* + past participle
*The goods **are packaged** automatically.*
*The parts **won't be delivered** on Monday.*
*When **is** the machine **being installed**?*

By can be used to include the agent.

*The machine was repaired **by the new fitter**.*

Use   **The passive is used in the following ways.**

- when the agent is unimportant or unknown
  *The product line **has been cleaned** and **checked**.*
- to describe systems and processes
  *The invoices **are dated**, **stamped** and **filed** in this cabinet.*
- to create an impersonal or formal style
  *I regret to inform you that several items **have been damaged** in transit.*

Conditionals (real possibility)

Form   **Conditionals (real possibility) have the following forms.**

if + present tense, present tense
*If it **breaks** down, we **mend** it straight away.*
if + present tense, modal verb + infinitive
*If we **fall** behind schedule, we'll **have to** work overtime.*

Use   **Conditionals (real possibility) are used in the following ways.**

- to show cause and effect
  *If we **increase** the sample rate, we **get** more rejects.*
- to predict the effect of an action
  *It's **going to increase** our costs if we **start** working overtime.*
- to request action if something happens
  ***Call** me if the components **don't arrive** today.*

Note!   ***If* introduces a possible event. *When* introduces an event that will definitely happen.**

*Ask her to call me **if** you see her.* (The person might see her.)

*Ask her to call me **when** you see her.* (The person will definitely see her.)

Grammar practice

Passive **1** **Match the sentence halves.**

1 The goods damaged in the fire   **a)** was installed last week.
2 The budget was based on costings that   **b)** were thrown away.
3 We're using the new machine that   **c)** were done last quarter.
4 The cars are painted by robots that   **d)** was recommended to us by Tom.
5 Our delivery company   **e)** have been checked by Maintenance.
6 We're only allowed to use machines that   **f)** are controlled by computers.

2 **Rewrite the sentences using the correct form of the passive.**

1 We installed the new machines last week.
   The new machines were installed last week.

2 Quality Control checks the products every fifteen minutes.
   _____

3 The supplier didn't deliver the machine parts this morning.
   _____

4 The manufacturer makes the products in Taiwan.
   _____

5 We don't assemble the final products here.
   _____

6 When did you last clean the production lines?
   _____

Conditionals **3** **Complete the sentences with the correct form of the verbs in brackets.**

1 If the warehouse (*be*) _____is_____ full, we usually (*store*) _____store_____ new produce in the factory itself.

2 We (*not / meet*) _____ our production target unless we ask some of the workers to work overtime.

3 If the parts (*be*) _____ out of stock, (*try*) _____ RT Supplies.

4 We (*have to*) _____ stop the line immediately if there (*be*) _____ a problem with one of the packaging machines.

5 The machine (*stop*) _____ if the sensor (*get*) _____ dirty.

6 We (*not / increase*) _____ our capacity unless we (*get*) _____ some new machinery.

7 We (*reduce*) _____ stoppages if we (*train*) _____ our operators.

8 (*Contact*) _____ me if the problem (*get*) _____ worse.

Passive and **4** **Find and correct the mistake in each line of the instructions.**
conditionals

Instructions for starting CP200 conveyor

1	• Make sure the conveyor <u>connects</u> to the mains power supply.	_is connected_
2	• Make sure the mains power switch set to "OFF".	_____
3	• Make sure all sensors set to "RESTART".	_____
4	• Any object blocking the sensors must be remove.	_____
5	• Check that nothing jam in the conveyor mechanism.	_____
6	• Press "START". If nothing will happen, switch off the power and	_____
7	reset the sensors. Check the sensors aren't obstruct by anything.	_____
8	• Any damaged machinery should reported to Maintenance.	_____

Vocabulary practice

1 Complete the word diagram with the following verbs.

<del>install</del> weigh label repair inspect package mend dispatch
protect fix check prevent wrap fasten

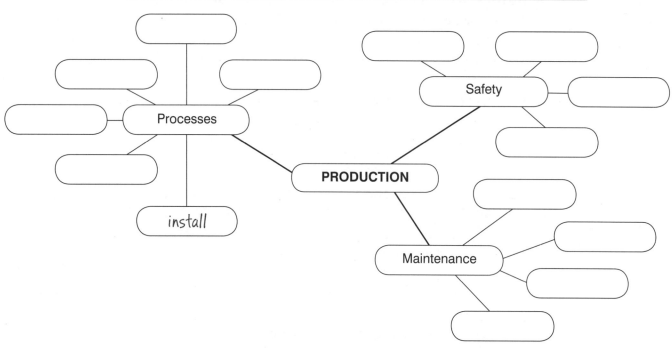

Processes

install

Safety

PRODUCTION

Maintenance

Word formation 2 Complete the table. Then use the words to complete the sentences below.

verb	noun
prevent	prevention
assemble	_____
_____	procedure
protect	_____
_____	construction
process	_____

1 A switch __prevented__ the machine from starting with the motor cover open.
2 The board has approved the new factory and _____ will start in July.
3 Once the line is shut down, we can _____ with the maintenance work.
4 We have just installed a new _____ line in the factory.
5 The whole production _____ takes 48 minutes from start to finish.
6 Our operatives have to wear eye _____ at all times.

Odd one out 3 Which word is the odd one out?

1 connect	join	separate	fasten
2 install	label	fit	load
3 operate	mend	fix	repair
4 combination	mix	method	junction
5 schedule	process	plan	organise
6 procedure	budget	costing	figures
7 dispatch	deliver	select	send
8 wrap	box	package	weigh

Multi-word verbs

4 Use the correct form of the following verbs to complete the sentences below.

> break down   cut out   shut down   key in
> start up   push through   turn on   burn out

1 We lost productivity on line four because the conveyor _broke down_ .
2 Don't forget to _____ the date on the labelling machine before you start.
3 The operator overloaded the machine and _____ the motor.
4 We have a safety routine before we _____ the assembly line in the morning.
5 The packaging machine _____ about 12,000 units a day.
6 We've had to _____ line three for emergency maintenance work.
7 The motors always _____ when they get too hot.
8 Make sure the power is _____ at the mains supply.

Production

5 Use the following words to complete the email below.

> assembly line   component   installation   machine
> operators   schedule   overload   adjustments

◄ ► email   RE: Nightshift report

From :   Mahendra Patel [mpatel@supersnacks.in]

Sent: Saturday, May 8, 2011 5:42 am
To: John Hopkins
Subject: RE: Nightshift report May 8

Nightshift report May 8
Shift manager: Ravi Singh

John
We had a few problems with ¹ _assembly line_ number two – mostly with the packaging ² _____ . Two motors burned out last night. The fitters have just finished the ³ _____ of the new motors. It took a while because they had problems getting a ⁴ _____ . Anyway, they're making some final ⁵ _____ and then it should be ready.

Could you tell your ⁶ _____ not to ⁷ _____ the machines as I think that's causing the problems. If we run the line at a steady 600 units per hour, we should still meet our production ⁸ _____ for the week.

Have a good shift.

Production jobs

6 Match the jobs with the sentences.

1 quality controller   a) 'We've inspected the sensors and they comply with the law.'
2 fitter   b) 'I'm going to need half a shift to work overtime on Saturday.'
3 machine operator   c) 'We're increasing the sample rate because of all the rejects.'
4 safety officer   d) 'It's going to take a couple of hours to install the new motor.'
5 production manager   e) 'I'm sorry but you need an identity card and safety clothing.'
6 security guard   f) 'If the line's running OK, there isn't really a lot for me to do.'

Financial services

Modal verbs (possibility)

Form **Modal verbs do not take -s, *to* or the auxiliary *do*.**

He cans transfer the money to your account today.
We should to review our insurance cover.
They don't can pay the bill. (They can't pay the bill.)

Use **These modal verbs are used in the following ways.**

- to express certainty (*must, will*)
  *He **must be** there by now.*
  *They **won't be ready** yet.*

- to express probability (*should, would*)
  *They **should be able** to transfer the money tomorrow.*
  *You **would save** money by banking online.*

- to express possibility (*may, might, can, could*)
  *A direct transfer **might be** quicker.*
  *I **could pay** by credit card.*

Gerunds (*-ing* forms)

Use **Gerunds are used in the following ways.**

- as nouns
  Exchanging *money is always expensive.*
  *There is an increase in the level of public **borrowing**.*

- after prepositions
  *I'm interested **in opening** an internet bank account.*
  *The company's been two months **without making** any repayments.*

- after certain verbs (see the list below)
  *I'm afraid you **keep going** over your credit limit.*
  *You can't **risk not insuring** your business premises.*

Here are some verbs often followed by a gerund.

admit	delay	go	mention	report
attempt	deny	hate	mind	risk
avoid	dislike	imagine	miss	start
begin	enjoy	keep	prefer	suggest
celebrate	face	like	postpone	
continue	finish	love	practise	

Grammar practice

Modal verbs   **1**   **Rewrite the following sentences using the modal verbs in brackets.**

1   It's possible the money won't arrive in time.
(*might*) <u>The money might not arrive in time.</u>

2   I'm sure internet banking is more profitable than running branches.
(*must*) _____

3   I think perhaps offshoring will save the banks a lot of money.
(*could*) _____

4   I don't expect the exchange rate to fall this week.
(*shouldn't*) _____

5   Perhaps labour costs will go up as the economy develops.
(*may*) _____

6   I can't believe the money is in the account yet.
(*won't*) _____

Gerunds   **2**   **Complete the sentences with the correct gerunds.**

~~advising~~   borrowing   insuring   lending   owing   repaying   withdrawing   debiting

1   We've started ___*advising*___ all our UK customers to quote prices in dollars.

2   The bank continued _____ them money despite their heavy debts.

3   We're trying to avoid _____ too much money from our company account.

4   They suggested _____ money from private investors to finance our plan.

5   We should think about _____ all our data against fire or theft.

6   The company denied _____ its creditors £400,000.

7   We should finish _____ the loan by the end of the year.

8   We've changed insurers, but they still keep _____ our account each month.

Gerunds and infinitives   **3**   **Complete the interview with the correct form of the verbs in brackets.**

Reporter   So, how do you like (¹*work*) ____*working*____ in a call centre?

Jan   It's OK, actually. It's not exactly what I planned (²*do*) _____
in life. But right now it's very convenient.

Reporter   How do you mean?

Jan   Well, I worked for an insurance company for a long time, but I finished (³*work*)
_____ there about a year ago to have a baby. I didn't really
enjoy (⁴*be*) _____ there any more, so I was more than happy
(⁵*be*) _____ a full-time mother and I certainly didn't want (⁶*go*)
_____ back to work there again. But I couldn't afford (⁷*not /
work*) _____ at all, so after about ten months I decided (⁸*look*)
_____ for a part-time job with flexible hours.

Reporter   So you came here …

Jan   Yes. The hours give me a way of (⁹*earn*) _____ some money
without (¹⁰*have*) _____ to pay for childcare during the day. I'll
probably continue (¹¹*work*) _____ for a few years. My husband
looks after our daughter while I'm at work in the evening or at the weekend.

Reporter   Does he mind (¹²*do*) _____ that?

Jan   No, not at all. He loves (¹³*be*) _____ on his own with her and I think
it's important for them (¹⁴*spend*) _____ time together. Of course,
we do miss (¹⁵*spend*) _____ time together as a family but we don't
really have much choice.

Vocabulary practice

Banking **1** **Use the following words to complete the website extract below.**

> ~~flexible~~ overdraft credited access deposit fee
> transfer funds balance interest branch

banking4u/home

Back Forward Reload Home Search Images Print Security Shop Stop

Location: http://www.banking4u.com   What's Related

contact us | help | customer | bank | invest | compare | shop

apply now

about us
who we are
sitemap
services
security
press centre
contact us

who we are

Banking4u offers a more ^{1} _flexible_ way of banking using the internet. As we don't have an expensive ^{2}_____ network to maintain, we are able to offer customers unbeatable ^{3}_____ on their savings. Our new EasyAccess account currently pays 5.45%. With our secure internet site you can ^{4}_____ money easily from one account to another at any time and with absolute peace of mind. What's more, any money you send will be ^{5}_____ to the recipient's account instantly and if the recipient is also a banking4u customer, there'll be no ^{6}_____ .

Customers also receive a debit card for convenient ^{7}_____ to their account when shopping. As the banking4u solution is based on a ^{8}_____ account only, we are currently unable to offer customers an ^{9}_____ facility. Therefore, customers will need to make sure they have sufficient ^{10}_____ in their account before they spend. Customers can check their ^{11}_____ at any time online.

Financial services **2** **Match the words. Then use them to complete the sentences below.**

financial——————bank
insurance ————services
exchange   card
fixed   agreement
service   policy
currency   rate
credit   exchange
central   term

1 _Financial services_ has been one of the real growth industries in the last fifteen years.
2 We took out an _____ against fire, flood and storm damage.
3 The US dollar – pound _____ is beginning to cause us concern.
4 I usually put all expenses on a company _____ when travelling on business.
5 We took out a loan for a _____ of ten years.
6 The European _____ has left the base rate on hold again this month.
7 Monthly statements and personal banking are part of our _____ .
8 The introduction of the euro should reduce our annual _____ costs.

Multi-word verbs

3 Match the multi-word verbs with the nouns.

1	insure against	debt / difficulties
2	sort out	fire / loss
3	fill in	shares / a company
4	invest in	a claims form / an application
5	get into	a problem / a disagreement

Confusables

4 Choose the correct word to complete each sentence.

1 The average credit card *debit / debt* in the UK is around £2,000.
2 We had to *borrow / lend* money from the bank to finance the expansion.
3 The 'creditors' section of a balance sheet shows what a company *owes / debts*.
4 The company gets a monthly *settlement / statement* from the bank.
5 The bank gets 1% currency exchange *surcharge / commission* on foreign transfers.
6 Most customers nowadays *deposit / withdraw* money from cash machines.
7 We took out a *loan / credit* with a 4% interest rate.
8 Our biggest single cost is the *hire / rent* we pay on our premises.

Job titles

5 Match the jobs with the duties.

1	bank clerk	**a)**	represents a company in court / gives legal advice
2	lawyer	**b)**	cashes cheques / exchanges currency / gives balances
3	personal banker	**c)**	transports documents and parcels quickly
4	investment banker	**d)**	sells policies / advises clients / assesses risk
5	insurance broker	**e)**	advises companies on buying stocks and shares
6	legal secretary	**f)**	assists lawyers / does research and general office duties
7	claims assessor	**g)**	advises on account management / sells banking products
8	courier	**h)**	decides on the level of insurance payouts

Word formation

6 Complete the table. Then use the correct form of the words to complete the sentences.

verb	noun
solve	solution
claim	_____
_____	repayment
insure	_____
_____	collection
support	_____
_____	advice
settle	_____

1 Banks are often an expensive __solution__ to the problem of raising capital.
2 We asked our _____ broker to find us the cheapest policy he could.
3 The bank provided financial _____ during our cash flow problems.
4 Our legal department _____ us on all copyright issues.
5 After all the floods, they processed our _____ very quickly.
6 Any debt unpaid for twelve months is transferred to a debt _____ agency.
7 We received a cheque to _____ the outstanding balance of the account.
8 The monthly _____ on the loan should finish in about three months' time.

International trade

Prepositions of time

Use *In* is used in the following ways.

- with periods of time (months, seasons, years)
  *We launched the product **in May** last year.*
  *I'm visiting Poland **in the summer**.*
  *The company started **in 2002**.*
- with parts of the day
  *I'll see you **in the morning** /**afternoon** /**evening***. (but **at night**)

At is used in the following ways.

- with times of the day
  *The meeting begins **at 10 o'clock**.*
  *I'll see you **at lunchtime**.*
- with events and festivals
  *We met **at the press launch**.*
  *I'm taking a few days off **at New Year**.*

On is used in the following ways.

- with days and dates
  *It should arrive **on Monday**.*
  *It was dispatched **on 16 June**.*
- with days and parts of the day
  *I'll do it **on Friday morning**.*

Obligation

Form The following verbs can be used to express obligation.

must   have to   need   should   ought to

Use These verbs can be used in the following ways.

- to express an obligation to do something
  *The contracts **must** be signed by 19 June.*
  *You **ought to** visit the supplier before we order from them.*
- to express an obligation not to do something
  *We **mustn't** start production until the contracts are signed.*
  *We **shouldn't** place too many orders with the same supplier.*
- to express a lack of obligation
  *You **needn't** send any more samples.*
  *We **don't have to** draw up the contracts until next month.*

Note! Both *must* and *have to* express positive obligation. However, the negative forms have different meanings. *Don't have to* is used to show something is not necessary.

*We **have to** / **must** deliver the goods by 31 October.*
*We **don't have to** /~~mustn't~~ work the same hours every day.*

Grammar practice

Prepositions **1 Write the times in the correct groups below.**

the 21st century	Saturday	Tuesday afternoon	11.45	2 August
Christmas	the last six months	the training seminar
February	spring	the 16th	2010	breakfast

in	at	on
the 21st century		

2 Complete the sentences with the correct preposition.

1 The company was registered __on__ 16 May 2003.

2 We last met _____ the Milan Trade Fair.

3 I hope to see you _____ Easter.

4 Business is usually quite quiet _____ the winter.

5 Imports rose by 3% _____ January.

6 The consignment is due to arrive in Hamburg _____ Saturday.

7 The shipment is due to arrive in Rotterdam _____ 18 September.

8 I don't think we'll have time _____ Friday afternoon.

9 We met him _____ Mr West's retirement party.

10 We broke several export records _____ 2011.

11 The courier should be here to pick the goods up _____ a couple of hours.

12 We even kept the office open _____ Christmas Day this year.

Obligation **3 Choose the correct option to complete each sentence.**

1 We ___mustn't___ let our quality levels fall on this important order.
   a) mustn't   **b)** needn't   **c)** ought to

2 All suppliers _____ comply with European standards if we use them.
   a) mustn't   **b)** must   **c)** ought to

3 You _____ speak Arabic to do business in the Middle East.
   a) mustn't   **b)** shouldn't   **c)** don't have to

4 We _____ take on any new orders that we can't produce in time.
   a) shouldn't   **b)** needn't   **c)** don't have to

5 Cultural differences _____ be a problem when doing business overseas.
   a) ought to   **b)** needn't   **c)** mustn't

6 Companies _____ ensure that suppliers can deliver on time.
   a) mustn't   **b)** needn't   **c)** must

7 We _____ place too many orders with one supplier.
   a) ought not to   **b)** needn't   **c)** don't have to

8 We _____ organise delivery – the customer will collect the goods.
   a) don't have to   **b)** shouldn't   **c)** mustn't

Vocabulary practice

1 Complete the word diagram with the following items related to transport.

~~cargo~~   ferry   harbour   motorway   airport   frontier   dock
lorry   highway   truck   air freight   railway   container ship   port
station   border   shipping   air terminal

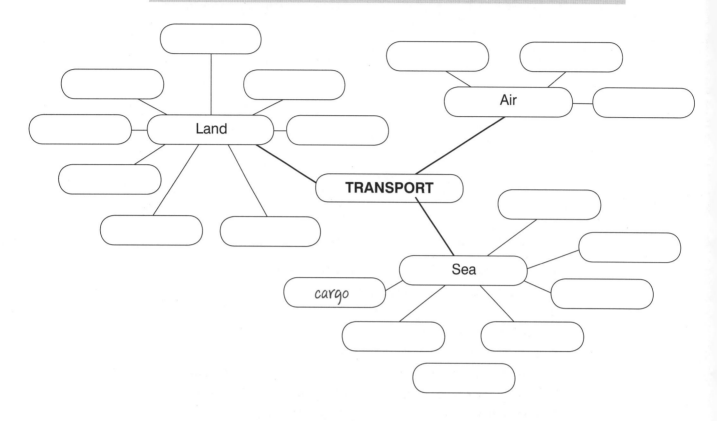

Importing **2** Put the following stages of an import process in the correct order.

- ☐ **a)** The import agent delivers the goods and invoices the customer.
- ☑ **b)** The customer places an order with the import agent.
- ☐ **c)** The import agent contacts a shipping company and arranges shipping.
- ☐ **d)** The supplier manufactures the goods.
- ☐ **e)** The goods clear customs and are loaded on board a ship.
- ☐ **f)** The import agent sends payment to the supplier.
- ☐ **g)** The import agent orders the goods from a supplier.
- ☐ **h)** The customer receives the goods and pays the import agent.
- ☐ **i)** The goods clear customs and are collected by the import agent.

Odd one out **3** Which word is the odd one out?

1	consignment	packet	parcel	instalment
2	duty	fee	margin	fare
3	distribution	dispatch	distance	delivery
4	discount	sale	offer	refund
5	schedule	timetable	itinerary	postage
6	deadline	fine	penalty	charge
7	invoice	permit	licence	visa
8	petrol	fuel	gasoline	litre

4 Use the following words to complete the dialogue below.

> ~~negotiations~~   deadlock   quality   quotation   bargain
> agreement   delay   consignment   quantity

Nancy   Lee, what happened with that new supplier you found?

Lee   I'm not sure. We're in ¹___negotiations___ with them right now and we've reached
²_____ – with no real progress, I'm afraid.

Nancy   You seemed quite excited about them a few weeks ago.

Lee   I was. I asked them for a ³_____ and the price they sent back looked
fantastic …

Nancy   But, don't tell me, the ⁴_____ was poor?

Lee   Not really. The sample products they sent looked good. For the price it looked like a
real ⁵_____ .

Nancy   So, what's the problem, then?

Lee   Well, they're quite a small company, so ⁶_____ would be a problem. They
wanted to deliver the jeans order in three parts, for example, one ⁷_____
every six weeks, but we're not keen on that. It would mean we'd have to
⁸_____ the launch of the winter catalogue, which we don't really
want to do.

Nancy   So, what are you going to do?

Lee   Well, if we don't reach an ⁹_____ soon, we'll just have to go back to our
usual suppliers. At least they're reliable.

5 Match the American English words with their British English equivalents.

US	UK
1 gasoline	cheque
2 check	post code
3 truck	motorway
4 zip	petrol
5 highway	lorry

6 Use the following phrases to complete the sentences below.

> ~~calculate prices~~   ban imports   list the contents   recycle packaging
> export goods   load the containers   cross the border   include delivery

1 Don't forget that when we _calculate prices_ , we always have to include import tax and a
handling fee for payments.

2 The government is trying to _____ to protect domestic manufacturers from a
flood of cheap foreign competition.

3 All the quoted prices are ex works and do not _____ or VAT.

4 It's safer for a company to _____ to its overseas markets than it is to invest large
amounts of money in setting up production facilities locally.

5 They managed to _____ on board two hours before the ship left Hamburg.

6 Make sure you _____ on this page of the shipping documents.

7 To reduce waste, we always try to _____ from the deliveries we receive from our
own suppliers.

8 The drivers had to wait twelve hours before they were finally allowed to _____
into Slovenia.

Recruitment

Conditionals (hypothetical situations)

Form | These conditionals have the following forms.

if + past tense, *would /could /might* + infinitive
*If we **advertised** online, we'**d get** more applicants.*
*We **could offer** more money if we **found** the right candidate.*
*If I **had** the right experience, I **might apply** for the job.*

Use | These conditionals are used in the following ways.

* to talk about hypothetical situations
  *If I **were** you, I'**d apply** for the job. (= I can't be you)*
  *I'm sure I'**d get** the job if I **spoke** German. (= I can't speak German)*
* to talk about actions we do not expect to happen
  *I'**d give** up my job if I **won** a million dollars.*
  *If we **recruited** several new people, we **wouldn't have to** work overtime.*

Note! | It is correct to use *were* for all hypothetical conditional forms of the verb *be*. However, *was* is also commonly used with *I /he /she /it*.

*If the company **weren't** so far away, I'd apply for the job.*
*If the company **wasn't** so far away, I'd apply for the job.*

A comma is used after, not before, the *if*-clause.

If they didn't like your CV, they wouldn't invite you for an interview.
They wouldn't invite you for an interview if they didn't like your CV.

Indirect questions

Form | Indirect questions have the following forms.

Yes /no questions (using *if /whether*)
*Could you tell me **if there are** any bonuses?*

Wh- questions
*Could you tell me **where you studied**, please?*

Indirect questions do not invert the subject and the verb and do not use the auxiliary verb *do*.

*Could you tell me **what** qualifications **you have**?*
*Could you tell me **what** qualifications ~~have you~~?*

*Could you tell me **when** you **left** university?*
*Could you tell me **when** ~~did you leave~~ university?*

Use | Indirect questions are used in the following way.

* to ask questions in a very polite or indirect way
  *Could you tell me **why you want** to change jobs?*
  *Could you tell me **what you think** about the idea?*

Grammar practice

Conditionals **1** **Use the information to write conditional sentences.**

1   I want to apply for the job but I don't have the right qualifications.
    If I had the right qualifications, I'd apply for the job.

2   We want to recruit more staff but we don't have the money.
    _____

3   I want to leave the company but the pay's so good.
    _____

4   We use an agency so it doesn't take months to fill a vacancy.
    _____

5   We're only able to run the office because we use temps.
    _____

6   Advertising on the internet is the only way of finding good IT people.
    _____

2 **Complete the sentences with the correct form of the verbs in brackets.**

1   I (*go*) _____'ll go_____ out and celebrate if I get the job.
2   I'd have a better chance if I (*speak*) _____ a little Chinese.
3   We'd save a lot of money if we (*not / use*) _____ a recruitment agency.
4   I think I'll apply for the manager's job if they (*advertise*) _____ it.
5   You (*not / meet*) _____ the deadline if you don't submit the application today.
6   I (*not / apply*) _____ for the job if the salary weren't so attractive.
7   We (*advertise*) _____ on our website if we (*not / find*) _____ a suitable internal applicant in the next couple of weeks.
8   I (*phone*) _____ and speak to the HR Officer if I (*be*) _____ you.
9   It (*be*) _____ great if I (*get*) _____ the job but I don't think I'm qualified enough.
10 You should hear from us within two weeks. If you (*not / do*) _____, then (*phone*) _____ our HR Manager, Mrs Al Belushi.
11 The interview went really well. I (*have to*) _____ take another day off work if they (*ask*) _____ me back for a second interview – which I think they will.
12 I'm not sure what I (*say*) _____ if they (*ask*) _____ me why I want to change jobs. It's one of those questions they always ask, isn't it?

Indirect questions **3** **Rewrite the direct questions as indirect questions.**

1   What are your duties at the moment?
    Could you tell me _what your duties are at the moment?_

2   What is your present salary?
    Could you tell me _____

3   Why did you leave your last job?
    Could you tell me _____

4   Do you speak any foreign languages?
    Could you tell me _____

5   How long were you in Switzerland?
    Could you tell me _____

6   Are you familiar with Windows 7?
    Could you tell me _____

7   Who did you work for in Brazil?
    Could you tell me _____

8   What did you like about the job?
    Could you tell me _____

Vocabulary practice

1 **Complete the word diagram with the following items related to job interviews.**

personal details   benefits   hobbies   qualifications   covering letter
salary   skills   career prospects   application form   referees
experience   certificates   holiday allowance

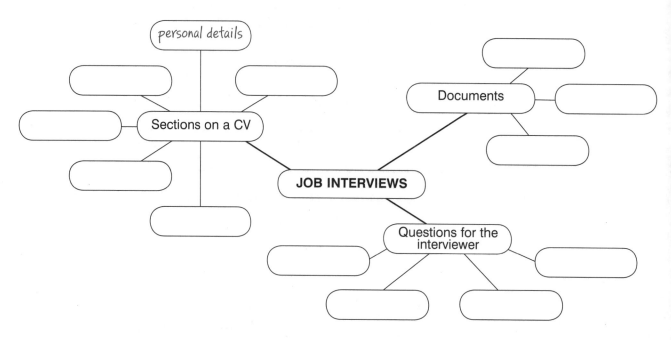

2 **Match the verbs with the nouns. Then use them in the correct form to complete the sentences below.**

apply for —— your resignation
turn down —— a job
take on   salary levels
select   vacancies
fill in   staff
review   a candidate
hand in   an offer
advertise   an application form

1   There's no way we can interview all the candidates who ___apply for a job___ .
2   Congratulations on the job offer. The boss is going to get a shock when you
_____ . I'd love to see his face when you do it!
3   We normally _____ from a shortlist of about four or five people.
4   The company's been doing very well recently and is now looking to expand and
_____ sometime early next year.
5   We're finding it very hard to keep our IT people at the moment, so I think we're going to
have to _____ to try and keep them with the company.
6   I got a letter from the Personnel Manager asking me to _____ and return it with
my CV and a photograph.
7   If it's for the Web Department, it's only really natural to _____ on the website.
That's where the people we need will be looking.
8   These days graduates can't afford to _____ . The job market is so competitive
that any job is worth considering.

Characteristics **3** **Match the personal characteristics with their definitions.**

1	bossy	**a)**	always makes time to assist colleagues
2	capable	**b)**	likes to tell others what to do
3	careful	**c)**	has done the job for many years
4	careless	**d)**	does not work very hard
5	cheerful	**e)**	does everything very well
6	confident	**f)**	is always happy at work
7	experienced	**g)**	makes a lot of mistakes
8	helpful	**h)**	always arrives on time
9	lazy	**i)**	does not worry about things being difficult
10	punctual	**j)**	tries very hard not to make mistakes

Word formation **4** **Complete the table. Then use the words to complete the sentences below.**

adjective	noun
skilled	_____skill_____
_____	absenteeism
ill	_____
punctual	_____
_____	anxiety
angry	_____
_____	qualifications
retired	_____

1 There seems to be a real shortage of ____skilled____ workers on the job market at the moment.

2 She was quite _____ during the interview. She looked very nervous.

3 You'll need to bring proof of your _____ to the interview – for example any certificates or diplomas.

4 We have a real _____ problem. We're losing about 200 working days a month with people being off work for one reason or another.

5 There's an infection going around the office so a lot of staff are off _____ .

6 Many people take early _____ in their 50s, creating a lot of vacancies.

7 We don't really have to worry about being _____ as the company operates a flexitime system.

8 I was really quite _____ when they told me in the interview that the job had already been given to someone else.

Personnel **5** **Match the words with a similar meaning.**

1	unemployed	**a)**	select
2	temporary	**b)**	evaluate
3	fire	**c)**	short-term
4	appoint	**d)**	pay
5	act	**e)**	dismiss
6	reward	**f)**	capable
7	assess	**g)**	behave
8	skilled	**h)**	out of work

Review unit 3 (13–17)

Grammar

1 Complete the sentences with the correct prepositions of time.

1 The interview is _____ 10.30 am.
2 The order is due for delivery _____ May.
3 I emailed her _____ Tuesday.
4 Employees get three extra days' holiday _____ Christmas.
5 The account was closed _____ 13 July.
6 I saw her _____ lunchtime.
7 The market has been very quiet _____ the last six months.
8 I'm meeting her _____ Saturday afternoon.

2 Rewrite the sentences using the correct form of the passive.

1 We credited the money to your account last week.
_____

2 The company buys its leisurewear from a supplier in Pakistan.
_____

3 Personnel posted the vacancy on the noticeboard this morning.
_____

4 We check all the goods when they arrive at the warehouse.
_____

5 Our legal department deals with late payments.
_____

6 When did you send the payment?
_____

7 They haven't loaded the consignment onto the ship yet.
_____

8 We didn't advertise the job internally.
_____

3 Complete the sentences with the correct conditional form.

1 If they (*not / confirm*) _____ the order soon, we (*have to*) _____ look for another customer.
2 I (*not / use*) _____ that supplier if I (*be*) _____ you.
3 We can't find a suitable candidate. And if we (*do*) _____ , we (*not / be able*) _____ to offer them enough money.
4 If we (*leave*) _____ the hotel at 5.40 tomorrow morning, I think we (*have to*) _____ ask for a wake up call at 4.30.
5 If a problem (*occur*) _____ with the machines, we always (*deal with*) _____ it immediately.
6 We (*improve*) _____ quality if we (*do*) _____ more testing, but we haven't got the staff to do it.
7 We (*increase*) _____ capacity if we (*have*) _____ enough money to buy new machinery.
8 If you (*need*) _____ any help, just (*call*) _____ me.

4 Rewrite the following sentences using the modal verbs in brackets.

1 There's a chance that the goods won't arrive in time.
   (might) _____

2 We've got no chance of finding good candidates locally.
   (won't) _____

3 Company policy requires us to advertise the position internally first.
   (have to) _____

4 We're not allowed to authorise payment until the goods have been checked.
   (can't) _____

5 I can't believe the money isn't in the account by now.
   (must) _____

6 We can lower our costs by ordering our goods from Sri Lanka.
   (would) _____

7 There's nothing in the contract about paying the invoice within thirty days.
   (have to) _____

8 Recruiting a full-time web designer would be a good idea.
   (should) _____

5 Complete the email with the correct form of the gerund or infinitive.

◄ ► email	RE: Sophie

From :	Andrew Thorpe [andrew.thorpe@ddl.de]
Sent:	Friday 18 May 14.27pm
To:	Kerstin Meyer
Subject:	**RE: Sophie**

Guess what? Sophie's just resigned! She's told me she just doesn't like (¹*work*) _____ here any more. I offered (²*raise*) _____ her salary but she still refused (³*stay*) _____. So, now we need (⁴*find*) _____ a new salesperson. What about (⁵*advertise*) _____ online? There's no point in (⁶*put*) _____ an ad in the local papers, is there? I've decided (⁷*begin*) _____ by (⁸*place*) _____ an ad on our own website. (⁹*find*) _____ someone for Sophie's position won't be easy, so I've asked her (¹⁰*work*) _____ the full notice period.

6 Rewrite the following as indirect questions beginning with *Could you tell me*.

1 'Who is your supplier?'
   Could you tell me _____ .

2 'Have you been offered the job yet?'
   Could you tell me _____ .

3 'How much did the shipping cost?'
   Could you tell me _____ .

4 Do you supply any of our competitors?'
   Could you tell me _____ .

5 'How long will the order take?'
   Could you tell me _____ .

6 'Where did you study?'
   Could you tell me _____ .

7 'Did the order arrive on time?'
   Could you tell me _____ .

8 'How much interest does the account pay?'
   Could you tell me _____ .

Vocabulary

Complete each sentence with the correct option.

1. Get an engineer in to ____mend____ the machine and get it running again.
   a) mend
   b) fasten
   c) construct

2. It's too big. It won't _____ into the container.
   a) package
   b) install
   c) fit

3. We arranged _____ at the bank to help us until our customers pay us.
   a) a deposit
   b) a transfer
   c) an overdraft

4. Could you just quickly _____ this form while you wait, please?
   a) label
   b) write
   c) fill in

5. Last year the port of Rotterdam was Europe's busiest _____ .
   a) dock
   b) terminal
   c) harbour

6. She seemed very _____ in the interview – very sure of herself.
   a) anxious
   b) careless
   c) confident

7. Many internet companies made a _____ last year.
   a) debt
   b) loss
   c) debit

8. We have regular health and safety training to help _____ accidents.
   a) process
   b) protect
   c) prevent

9. I returned the goods and asked them to _____ my money.
   a) reward
   b) replace
   c) refund

10. The goods are _____ in protective film before going to the warehouse.
    a) combined
    b) repaired
    c) wrapped

11. Make sure you get the customer's address and _____ .
    a) postcode
    b) postage
    c) direction

12. The higher fuel costs will start to reduce our _____ soon.
    a) prices
    b) margins
    c) schedules

13. It's important we recruit someone with the right _____ for the job.
    a) qualifications
    b) certificates
    c) studies

14. The new cooker's in the warehouse right now, ready for _____ next week.
    a) preparation
    b) production
    c) installation

15. Their interest _____ on loans are very low at the moment.
    a) rates
    b) terms
    c) policies

16. I'd like to make a _____ on my car insurance, please.
    a) claim
    b) settlement
    c) collection

17. The contract includes a _____ clause in case of late delivery.
    a) permit
    b) procedure
    c) penalty

18. If we _____ the two conveyors, they should reach the warehouse.
    a) fix
    b) join
    c) fasten

19. The order's really important so we'd better make it a _____ .
    a) deadline
    b) priority
    c) consignment

20. Everyone was shocked when she handed in her letter of _____ .
    a) resignation
    b) retirement
    c) recruitment

21. It took us three days to _____ a deal that was acceptable to both companies.
    a) calculate
    b) argue
    c) negotiate

22. Get some independent financial _____ before you take the loan.
    a) advice
    b) assessment
    c) support

23. We need to _____ them onto the lorry to make room in the warehouse.
    a) load
    b) weigh
    c) dispatch

24. They've had to _____ a lot of money from the bank this year.
    a) lend
    b) borrow
    c) credit

25. He's _____ and always telling people what to do.
    a) lazy
    b) bossy
    c) angry

26 The shipment should be crossing the _____ this evening.
   a) border   **b)** line   **c)** customs

27 We'll have to check our bank _____ to see what funds are available.
   a) invoice   **b)** reference   **c)** statement

28 I'd like to _____ $300 from my account, please.
   a) owe   **b)** withdraw   **c)** charge

29 The guests should arrive soon according to the _____ they sent.
   a) itinerary   **b)** distribution   **c)** deadline

30 Some countries charge high import _____ to protect domestic industry.
   a) fines   **b)** duties   **c)** fees

31 Air _____ has been steadily increasing due to problems with the railways.
   a) dispatch   **b)** shipping   **c)** freight

32 I'd like to apply for the _____ advertised on the website last week.
   a) vacancy   **b)** prospect   **c)** application

33 To sell off all our old stock, we gave customers a _____ of 50%.
   a) penalty   **b)** discount   **c)** refund

34 The project was 5% below _____ , saving the company 22,000 euros.
   a) figures   **b)** budget   **c)** procedure

35 Our brokers get a generous _____ on everything they sell.
   a) repayment   **b)** commission   **c)** agreement

36 If the payments don't arrive soon, the account will go into _____ .
   a) debit   **b)** credit   **c)** debt

37 All wage levels are _____ on an annual basis.
   a) appointed   **b)** selected   **c)** reviewed

38 Our top five customers get a 40% _____ on orders over $100,000.
   a) discount   **b)** deal   **c)** distribution

39 We _____ the machines every day for faults or signs of wear.
   a) prevent   **b)** inspect   **c)** repair

40 I keep my savings in a high interest _____ account.
   a) debt   **b)** debit   **c)** deposit

41 They agreed to ship the order for printing machines in three _____ .
   a) parcels   **b)** quantities   **c)** consignments

42 He's very _____ not to make any mistakes when doing the accounts.
   a) careful   **b)** cheerful   **c)** capable

43 The bank said there weren't enough _____ in the account.
   a) deposits   **b)** contents   **c)** funds

44 The machine _____ will need training on the new packaging machines.
   a) operator   **b)** guard   **c)** controller

45 There's a 1% commission on all foreign currency _____ .
   a) exchanges   **b)** surcharges   **c)** balances

46 The cheapest way is by road and across the Channel on a passenger _____ .
   a) container   **b)** truck   **c)** ferry

47 She _____ her resignation shortly after the merger was completed.
   a) handed in   **b)** dismissed   **c)** turned down

48 The bank is closing a lot of its high street _____ and going onto the internet.
   a) shops   **b)** branches   **c)** offices

49 We'll need to get an import _____ before we're allowed to sell there.
   a) acceptance   **b)** visa   **c)** licence

50 The _____ on our Shanghai offices has risen sharply over the last two years.
   a) rent   **b)** hire   **c)** tax

Writing

Emails

1 A UK manager writes to a US colleague about selling her products in the USA. Look at their emails on the opposite page and put them in the order in which they were written. What helped you put them in order?

2 Look at the way the emails open and close and fill in the table.

openings	closings
Dear Mr Laws	

Now put the lists into an order of formality, from the most formal openings and closings to the least formal.

3 Look at the emails again and read the following statements about email. Do you agree or disagree with them?

1 Emails are always less formal than letters.

2 Emails are usually shorter than letters.

3 Emails often use short forms (e.g. *I'd, it's, they're*).

4 Emails don't always need an opening (e.g. *Dear Mr Laws*).

4 Look at the following email. Rewrite it to make it less formal. Then write an informal reply to it.

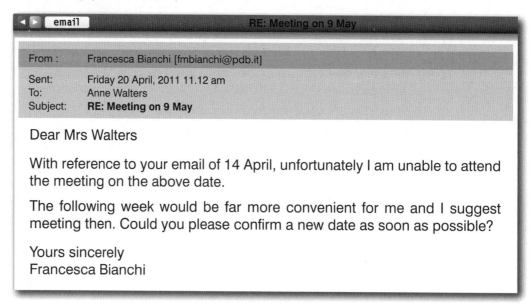

email | RE: Meeting on 9 May

From : Francesca Bianchi [fmbianchi@pdb.it]
Sent: Friday 20 April, 2011 11.12 am
To: Anne Walters
Subject: **RE: Meeting on 9 May**

Dear Mrs Walters

With reference to your email of 14 April, unfortunately I am unable to attend the meeting on the above date.

The following week would be far more convenient for me and I suggest meeting then. Could you please confirm a new date as soon as possible?

Yours sincerely
Francesca Bianchi

A

Dear Mr Laws

Marjorie Osbourne has asked me to contact you regarding our new range of Biosoaps. I am the Brand Manager for the Shampoo and Soaps Division and I would be interested to know whether you think there might be any potential for selling the Biosoap range in our US markets.

If you are interested, I would like to forward a sample of the Biosoap range along with some new product information.

I look forward to hearing from you soon.

Yours sincerely

Joyce Campbell
Brand Manager
Soaps and Shampoo Division

B

Joyce

Tuesday's great. The meeting's Thursday, so that's perfect. I'll email you any ideas my sales reps have for adapting the product.

I look forward to sharing the product with my team.

All the best
Charles

C

Dear Charles

Thanks for the quick reply. The samples are in the post and should get to you by Tuesday. I hope it's in time for your sales meeting.

We'd also be grateful for any feedback on how to adapt the product for US markets.

Regards
Joyce

D

Many thanks. I look forward to your comments.

Joyce

E

Dear Joyce

Thanks for your email. I'd be happy to look at the Biosoap samples and show them to my reps at our sales meeting next week.

When would you be able to get them here?

Kind regards
Charles

Formal letters

1 Read the letter below and the tips on how to write formal letters.

On headed paper, start the letter with the name and address of the person you are writing to.

Always date the letter.

Use a reference line to say what the subject of the letter is.

Always use an appropriate opening. (See opposite.)

If there has been previous contact, refer to it.

Always set the letter out in clear paragraphs.

Short forms, e.g. *we'd* or *don't* are not normally used in formal letters.

Always use an appropriate closing. (See opposite.)

Sign the letter. Type your name and job title.

cc the names of anyone who will also receive a copy of the letter.

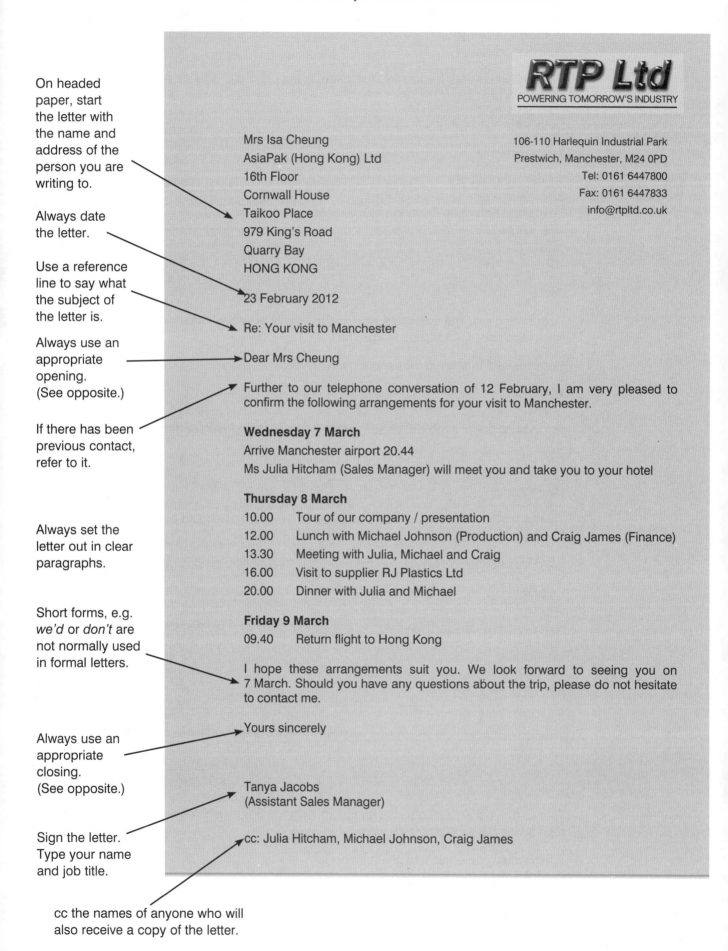

RTP Ltd
POWERING TOMORROW'S INDUSTRY

106-110 Harlequin Industrial Park
Prestwich, Manchester, M24 0PD
Tel: 0161 6447800
Fax: 0161 6447833
info@rtpltd.co.uk

Mrs Isa Cheung
AsiaPak (Hong Kong) Ltd
16th Floor
Cornwall House
Taikoo Place
979 King's Road
Quarry Bay
HONG KONG

23 February 2012

Re: Your visit to Manchester

Dear Mrs Cheung

Further to our telephone conversation of 12 February, I am very pleased to confirm the following arrangements for your visit to Manchester.

Wednesday 7 March
Arrive Manchester airport 20.44
Ms Julia Hitcham (Sales Manager) will meet you and take you to your hotel

Thursday 8 March
10.00	Tour of our company / presentation
12.00	Lunch with Michael Johnson (Production) and Craig James (Finance)
13.30	Meeting with Julia, Michael and Craig
16.00	Visit to supplier RJ Plastics Ltd
20.00	Dinner with Julia and Michael

Friday 9 March
09.40   Return flight to Hong Kong

I hope these arrangements suit you. We look forward to seeing you on 7 March. Should you have any questions about the trip, please do not hesitate to contact me.

Yours sincerely

Tanya Jacobs
(Assistant Sales Manager)

cc: Julia Hitcham, Michael Johnson, Craig James

2 Here are some useful phrases when writing letters.

Openings
Dear Sir / Madam
Dear Mr Laws
Dear Mrs Marcolini
Dear Michael

Closings
Yours faithfully
Yours sincerely
Kind / Best regards
Regards

Referring to previous contact
With reference to your letter of …
Further to our phone call of …
Thank you for your enquiry of …
Thank you for your email yesterday.

Enclosures / attachments
Please find the attached …
I enclose the …
I have attached a …
Here is the …

Requesting
We would be very grateful if you could …
Could you please …
Would it be possible to …
Could we …

Offering
If you require any assistance, …
We are able to offer …
We could …
Would you like us to …

Confirming
As discussed, …
As agreed, …

Suggesting / recommending
May I suggest …
We should …

Complaining
I would like to complain about the …

Apologising
We apologise for …
We are sorry about the …

Finishing a letter
If you have any further questions, please do not hesitate to contact us.
We look forward to seeing / meeting you on …
I look forward to hearing from you.

3 Read the following email from a colleague and write a suitable letter of reply.

> Gill ·
>
> I'm on holiday next week so could I ask a favour? I need to reply to a letter I got yesterday from a company called Network Schweiz – an IT service company looking for new business. Could you write back to them for me, ask for a price list and make an appointment for one of their people to come and see us some time when I'm back? The woman who wrote to me is Anja Ratzenberger. Her address is:
>
> Network Schweiz
> Neunbrunnenstr 18
> 8050 Zurich
> Switzerland

Answer key (Units 1–17)

Unit 1: Jobs

Grammar practice

1 2 check
3 spend
4 don't leave
5 doesn't have
6 Do you work
7 deals
8 Does your job involve

2 2 Where does he work?
3 When do you (usually) have lunch?
4 What kind of computers do they use?
5 How does she travel to work?
6 Who do you report to?
7 How often does your boss go to Head Office?

3 2 We rarely receive telephone calls.
3 The bonuses are always late.
4 We don't often leave the office until 7.30.
5 All the managers meet annually in Prague.

4 2 involves
3 ✓
4 often spend
5 works
6 doesn't know
7 always look
8 spends
9 can't / cannot
10 ✓

Vocabulary practice

1
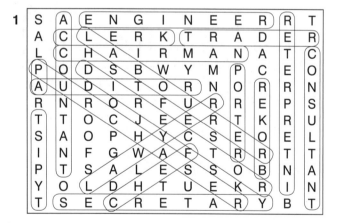

2 operator   operate   **operation**
supervisor   **supervise**   supervision
assessor   assess   assessment
co-ordinator   **co-ordinate**   **co-ordination**
inspector   **inspect**   inspection

2 inspector
3 assessment
4 operation
5 co-ordination
6 supervise

3 1 trade union
2 holidays
3 bonuses
4 retirement
5 pension
6 salary
7 illness
8 working hours

4 1 DS
2 R
3 W
4 DS
5 DS
6 W
7 DS
8 W

Unit 2: Companies

Grammar practice

1 2 established
3 started
4 named
5 became
6 increased
7 came
8 grew
9 didn't begin
10 merged
11 expanded
12 was
13 appointed
14 made
15 announced

2 2 's it going
3 's getting
4 Are you selling
5 aren't selling
6 are looking
7 are you staying
8 'm not flying
9 are you attending
10 'm looking
11 's asking

3 2 wants
3 have
4 manufacture
5 launches
6 doesn't believe
7 're taking
8 are you going
9 think
10 are rising

4 2 wasn't
3 did they set up
4 didn't allow
5 did you locate
6 did the bank reject
7 didn't think
8 didn't they stay

Vocabulary practice

1 2 get funding
3 draw up a business plan
4 locate premises
5 recruit staff
6 set up a company
7 invest in equipment
8 make / made a profit

2 1 automobile
2 publishing
3 agriculture
4 manufacturing
5 banking
6 telecommunications

3 2 wholesaler
3 plant
4 subsidiary
5 rivals
6 Personnel

4 2 break up
3 monopoly
4 division
5 agriculture
6 sales
7 produce
8 specialise

72 **Answer key**

Unit 4: Communication

Grammar practice

1 a   2 b   3 b   4 a

2 May/Can I help
3 Can/Could/Would you give
4 I'll just get
5 May/Can/Could I ask
6 Can/Could/Would you tell
7 can't make
8 have to attend
9 I'll give
10 Can/Could/Would you make
11 mustn't/can't print
12 I'll check
13 Can/Could you hold
14 Should/Shall I call
15 Can/Could you call
16 I'll get

Vocabulary practice

1
1 Unfortunately
2 However
3 instead of
4 unless
5 whether
6 while

2
2 enclosed
3 grateful
4 afraid
5 inconvenience
6 attention
7 regret
8 contact
9 enquiry
10 insist

3
2 fill in a form
3 write down some information
4 hang up the phone
5 cross out a mistake

4
1 estimate
2 note
3 apologies
4 postponed
5 requested
6 in case
7 remind
8 refused

5
2 e
3 g
4 a
5 h
6 f
7 d
8 c

6
1 postpone
2 request
3 recommend
4 confirm
5 apologise
6 complain

Unit 5: Performance

Grammar practice

1
2 well
3 steadily
4 late
5 monthly
6 hard
7 dramatically
8 fast

2
2 slight
3 dramatic
4 strongly
5 suddenly
6 good
7 well
8 steady
9 sharp
10 strong

3
2 got
3 did we do
4 still haven't sent
5 has sent
6 did
7 beat
8 did they manage
9 were
10 was
11 won
12 haven't heard

Vocabulary practice

1

positive	neutral	negative
beat	break even	fail
ahead	on target	behind
overtake		disappointing

2
2 savings
3 opportunity
4 achievement
5 acquisition
6 expansion
7 recovery
8 announcement

3
2 prediction
3 profit
4 value
5 result
6 previous
7 project
8 position

4 flow chart (a): 3
bar chart (b): 1, 4, 6, 7
graph (c): 1, 4, 6, 7
pie chart (d): 2, 5, 8

5
2 f
3 e
4 a
5 c
6 d

6
2 We produce locally because of (the) lower production costs.
3 Trading in euros means (that) we've had to update all our systems.
4 Problems with a supplier caused delivery delays.
5 Rising production costs are leading to smaller margins.
6 European exports have risen due to a fall in the value of the euro.
7 It will be easier to distribute directly to customers because of an increase in internet usage.
8 New regulations will lead to an increase in our export business.

Unit 7: Products

Grammar practice

1
2 more powerful
3 fastest
4 most modern
5 best
6 easier
7 smaller
8 most competitive

2
1 'm leaving
2 does the plane land
    lands

3 are we meeting
  'll meet
4 'll send
5 are going to be
6 are the press arriving
7 leaves
  'll just call
8 're going to update
9 are you going to call
  're doing
10 are bringing out
  're bringing forward

Vocabulary practice

1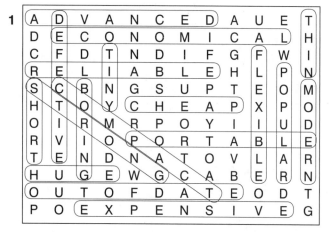

2 accurate   inaccurate   accuracy
  available   **unavailable**   **availability**
  capable   incapable   **capability**
  flexible   **inflexible**   flexibility
  comfortable   **uncomfortable**   **comfort**
  convenient   inconvenient   convenience
  efficient   **inefficient**   **efficiency**
  popular   **unpopular**   popularity

3 1 guarantee   5 non-standard
  2 return   6 customer service
  3 condition   7 replacement
  4 wear and tear   8 consumer

4 long   **length**   centimetres / metres
  wide   width   **centimetres / metres**
  deep   **depth**   centimetres / metres
  fast   **speed**   kilometres per hour
  heavy   **weight**   kilogrammes

5 2 portable   6 boring
  3 out of date   7 attractive
  4 economical   8 strong
  5 defective

Unit 8: Office equipment

Grammar practice

1 2 dial   6 tick
  3 Don't email   7 Don't phone
  4 file   8 Delete
  5 Don't stop

2 **countable nouns**   **uncountable nouns**
  catalogue   information
  email   stationery
  program   support
  price   equipment
  diary   hardware
  network   money
                       news
                       stock

3 2 a lot of / many   7 stationery
  3 a lot of /much   8 little
  4 many /a lot / any   9 work /a job
  5 some   10 any
  6 few

Vocabulary practice

1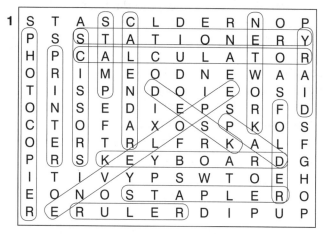

2 2 air-conditioning   6 filing cabinet
  3 word processor   7 memory stick
  4 price list   8 rubber stamp
  5 paper clip

3 2 Switch off the computer
  3 fill up the paper tray
  4 print out a report
  5 fill in the/an order form
  6 run out of toner
  7 take away the faulty machine

4 **documents**   **computers**   **problems**
  quotation   hardware   out of order
  form   memory   defective
  invoice   program   out of stock
  guarantee   cable   faulty
  receipt
  service agreement

1 cable	4 order
2 central heating	5 bulb
3 supplier	6 sheets

Unit 10: Business travel

Grammar practice

2	d	6	f
3	a	7	h
4	e	8	g
5	c		

2 She promised not to book that hotel again.
3 She reminded me to take the new brochures.
4 She warned me not to go into the east part of the city at night.
5 She refused to do the report.
6 She asked me not to take next week off.

2 I see AirEast is going to launch an executive class.
3 I see Shanghai hotel prices are going to go up.
4 I see Stansted airport is going to expand.
5 I see the euro isn't going to recover against the dollar in the near future.
6 I see the strike is going to hit the London underground.

Vocabulary practice

2	check-in desk	6	passport control
3	excess baggage	7	customs officer
4	boarding card	8	duty-free shops
5	departure lounge	9	information board

2
meat	fish	fruit	veg. / salad
lamb	cod	orange	onion
sausage	plaice	pear	peas
chicken		strawberry	potato
bacon			pepper
turkey			corn
pork			lettuce
			mushroom
			carrot
			spinach
			celery
			cauliflower

3
1	reservation	6	parking
2	fortnight	7	plug in
3	non-smoking	8	mini-bar
4	balcony	9	bill
5	breakfast	10	check out

4
2 plug in a computer
3 check out of a hotel
4 take off a jacket
5 get on a plane
6 check in at the airport

5
1	shirt	6	shoes
2	suitcase	7	jacket
3	trousers	8	suit
4	tie	9	overcoat
5	jackets		

Unit 11: Conferences

Grammar practice

1
2	d	4	e	6	f
3	c	5	a		

2
2 'll serve, finish / have finished
3 make / have made, 'll have
4 'll book / 's going to book, receives / has received
5 'll check / 'm going to check, start
6 know, aren't going to book / won't book
7 'll have to / have to, starts
8 finish / have finished, 'll be / 's going to be

3
3	the	8	a	13	the
4	Ø	9	the	14	the
5	the	10	a	15	the
6	Ø	11	the		
7	a	12	Ø		

Vocabulary practice

1
2	speech	8	launch
3	Presentation	9	show
4	break	10	tea
5	seminar	11	delegates
6	sandwiches	12	stand
7	refreshments		

2
person	verb	noun
speaker	speak	**speech**
specialist	**specialise**	specialisation
attendee	**attend**	**attendance**
promoter	promote	**promotion**
presenter	**present**	**presentation**
guide	**guide**	guide
host/ess	**host**	hosting

2	specialists	6	speech / presentation
3	hosting	7	speech / presentation
4	attended	8	guide
5	promoter		

3
1	trade fair	5	advance booking
2	attend	6	venue
3	bring forward	7	invitations
4	rearrange	8	crowded

4
1	buffet lunch	4	dining room
2	shower	5	bathroom
3	lift	6	dry-cleaning

Unit 13: Processes

Grammar practice

1 1 b   3 a   5 d
    2 c   4 f   6 e

2 2 The products are checked every fifteen minutes.
    3 The machine parts weren't delivered this morning.
    4 The products are made in Taiwan.
    5 The final products aren't assembled here.
    6 When were the production lines last cleaned?

3 2 won't meet
    3 are, try
    4 have to / 'll have to, is
    5 stops / 'll stop, gets
    6 won't increase / aren't going to increase, get
    7 'll reduce, train
    8 Contact, gets

4 2 is set   6 happens
    3 are set   7 obstructed
    4 removed   8 be reported
    5 is jammed

Vocabulary practice

1

processes	safety	maintenance
weigh	inspect	repair
label	protect	mend
package	check	fix
dispatch	prevent	fasten
wrap		

2

verb	noun
assemble	**assembly**
proceed	procedure
protect	**protection**
construct	construction
process	**process**

    2 construction   5 process
    3 proceed   6 protection
    4 assembly

3 1 separate   5 process
    2 label   6 procedure
    3 operate   7 select
    4 method   8 weigh

4 2 key in   6 shut down
    3 burnt / burned out   7 cut out
    4 start up   8 turned on
    5 pushes through

5 2 machine   6 operators
    3 installation   7 overload
    4 component   8 schedule
    5 adjustments

6 1 c   3 f   5 b
    2 d   4 a   6 e

Unit 14: Financial services

Grammar practice

1 2 Internet banking must be more profitable …
    3 Offshoring could save the banks a lot …
    4 The exchange rate shouldn't fall …
    5 Labour costs may go up as the economy …
    6 The money won't be in the account …

2 2 lending   6 owing
    3 withdrawing   7 repaying
    4 borrowing   8 debiting
    5 insuring

3 2 to do   7 not to work   12 doing
    3 working   8 to look   13 being
    4 being   9 earning   14 to spend
    5 to be   10 having   15 spending
    6 to go   11 working

Vocabulary practice

1 2 branch   6 fee   10 funds
    3 interest   7 access   11 balance
    4 transfer   8 deposit
    5 credited   9 overdraft

2 2 insurance policy   6 Central Bank
    3 exchange rate   7 service agreement
    4 credit card   8 currency exchange
    5 fixed term

3 2 sort out a problem / a disagreement
    3 fill in a claims form / an application
    4 invest in shares / a company
    5 get into debt / difficulties

4 1 debt   5 commission
    2 borrow   6 withdraw
    3 owes   7 loan
    4 statement   8 rent

5 2 a   4 e   6 f   8 c
    3 g   5 d   7 h

6

verb	noun
claim	**claim**
repay	repayment
insure	**insurance**
collect	collection
support	**support**
advise	advice
settle	**settlement**

2 insurance
3 support
4 advised
5 claim

6 collection
7 settle
8 repayments

Unit 16: International trade

Grammar practice

in: the last six months, February, spring, 2010
at: 11.45, Christmas, the training seminar, breakfast
on: Saturday, Tuesday afternoon, 2 August, the 16th

2	at	6	on	10	in
3	at	7	on	11	in
4	in	8	on	12	on
5	in	9	at		

| 2 | b | 4 | a | 6 | c | 8 | a |
| 3 | c | 5 | b | 7 | a | | |

Vocabulary practice

land	air	sea
motorway	airport	ferry
frontier	air freight	harbour
lorry	air terminal	dock
highway		container ship
truck		port
railway		shipping
station		
border		

2 b – g – d – c – f – e – i – a – h

3 1 instalment
2 margin
3 distance
4 refund

5 postage
6 deadline
7 invoice
8 litre

4 2 deadlock
3 quotation
4 quality
5 bargain

6 quantity
7 consignment
8 delay
9 agreement

5 1 gasoline / petrol
2 check / cheque
3 truck / lorry

4 zip / post code
5 highway / motorway

6 2 ban imports
3 include delivery
4 export goods
5 load the containers

6 list the contents
7 recycle packaging
8 cross the border

Unit 17: Recruitment

Grammar practice

1 2 We'd recruit more staff if we had the money.
3 I'd leave the company if the pay weren't so good.
4 It'd take months to fill a vacancy if we didn't use an agency.

5 We wouldn't be able to run the office if we didn't use temps.
6 We wouldn't be able to find good IT people if we didn't advertise on the internet.

2 2 spoke
3 didn't use
4 advertise
5 won't meet
6 wouldn't apply
7 'll advertise, don't find

8 'd phone, were / was
9 'd be, got
10 don't, phone
11 'll have to, ask
12 'll say / 'm going to say, ask

3 2 … what your present salary is?
3 … why you left your last job?
4 … if / whether you speak any foreign languages?
5 … how long you were in Switzerland?
6 … if / whether you are familiar with …
7 … who you worked for in Brazil?
8 … what you liked about the job?

Vocabulary practice

1
CV sections	documents	questions
hobbies	covering letter	benefits
skills	application form	salary
referees	certificates	career prospects
experience		holiday allowance
qualifications		

2 2 hand in your resignation
3 select a candidate
4 take on staff
5 review salary levels

6 fill in an application form
7 advertise vacancies
8 turn down an offer

3	2	e	5	f	8	a
	3	j	6	i	9	d
	4	g	7	c	10	h

4
adjective	noun
absent	absenteeism
ill	**illness**
punctual	**punctuality**
anxious	anxiety
angry	**anger**
qualified	qualifications
retired	**retirement**

2 anxious
3 qualifications
4 absenteeism
5 ill

6 retirement
7 punctual
8 angry

| 5 | 1 | h | 3 | e | 5 | g | 7 | b |
| | 2 | c | 4 | a | 6 | d | 8 | f |

Answer key (Reviews 1–3)

Review 1 (Units 1–5)

Grammar

1
1. 'm writing
2. are arriving
3. want
4. 's preparing
5. are your visitors arriving
6. think
7. has
8. don't have
9. takes
10. Does Mandy know

2
1. 'll
2. May
3. have to
4. mustn't
5. shouldn't
6. can
7. May
8. could
9. Shall
10. Could

3
2. dramatic
3. extremely
4. slight
5. steadily
6. steadily
7. quickly
8. sharp
9. steadily
10. steady

4
2. had
3. haven't all come
4. sent
5. got / 've got
6. 've already asked
7. didn't all arrive
8. Did you mention
9. were
10. 's always been
11. 've arranged / arranged
12. haven't come
13. saw
14. went
15. told
16. 's just come
17. made
18. promised
19. didn't tell
20. haven't even started

Vocabulary

1. b) interpreter
2. c) secretary
3. c) turnover
4. a) member
5. c) bonus
6. c) chairman
7. c) manufacturing
8. a) headquarters
9. c) wholesaler
10. c) memo
11. b) whether
12. a) remind
13. c) cross out
14. b) beaten
15. c) budget
16. a) growth
17. a) operator
18. c) overtime
19. a) pension
20. c) set up
21. a) parent company
22. b) merger
23. c) Personnel
24. c) Therefore
25. c) call back
26. c) confirm
27. b) invoice
28. b) reduce
29. b) expansion
30. a) forecast
31. b) sharply
32. c) fall
33. a) chatted
34. b) announced
35. b) agenda
36. b) inconvenient
37. c) grateful
38. a) complaints
39. c) unless
40. b) attached
41. c) ask
42. b) sales
43. a) membership
44. a) located
45. c) rivals
46. c) running
47. c) inconvenience
48. b) instead
49. a) brands
50. c) recent

Review 2 (Units 7–11)

Grammar

1
1. 're flying
2. arrives
3. are the guests arriving
4. need / 'll need / 're going to need
5. leave
6. 'll call
7. won't manage / aren't going to manage
8. finish / have finished
9. 're not going / aren't going
10. I'll send

2
1. a) a few
2. b) any
3. b) a few
4. c) some
5. b) many
6. c) any
7. c) some
8. a) a few
9. c) many
10. c) a few
11. b) a little
12. a) some
13. b) a few
14. c) a little
15. b) any

3
2. the most expensive
3. the worst
4. friendlier than
5. cheaper than
6. more economical than
7. fast as
8. the most convenient
9. worse
10. as large

1 the
2 the
3 the
4 The
5 the
6 Ø
7 an
8 Ø
9 The
10 the
11 a
12 an
13 the
14 a
15 a

Vocabulary

1 a) efficient
2 b) design
3 b) portable
4 a) fall off
5 a) quotations
6 c) wide
7 a) switch
8 c) cables
9 b) stock
10 a) fill in
11 c) delete
12 a) network
13 c) guarantee
14 c) briefcase
15 b) takes off
16 c) excess
17 a) turkey
18 c) shirt
19 b) plug
20 c) flight
21 b) boarding card
22 a) delegates
23 c) hungry
24 c) launch
25 a) buffet
26 b) venue
27 c) convenient
28 b) boring
29 a) reliable
30 b) measurements
31 a) stamp
32 c) install
33 a) supplies
34 b) envelope
35 b) IT
36 c) memory
37 b) unavailable
38 a) cod
39 b) reception
40 b) bulb
41 b) diary
42 a) invitation
43 b) fill in
44 c) speech
45 c) strawberries
46 a) returns
47 a) stand
48 c) forward
49 a) lounge
50 c) tights

Review 3 (Units 13–17)

Grammar

1 at
2 in
3 on
4 at
5 on
6 at
7 in
8 on

2 1 The money was credited to your account …
2 Their leisurewear is bought from a supplier …
3 The vacancy was posted on the noticeboard …
4 All the goods are checked when they arrive …
5 Late payments are dealt with by our legal …
6 When was the payment sent?
7 The consignment hasn't been loaded onto …
8 The job wasn't advertised internally.

3 1 don't confirm, 'll have to
2 wouldn't use, were
3 did, wouldn't be able
4 leave, 'll have to
5 occurs, deal with
6 'd improve, did
7 'd increase, had
8 need, call

4 1 The goods might not arrive in time.
2 We won't find good candidates locally.
3 We have to advertise the position internally …
4 We can't authorise payment until the goods …
5 The money must be in the account by now.
6 We'd lower our costs by ordering our goods …
7 We don't have to pay the invoice within thirty days.
8 We should recruit a full-time web designer.

5 1 working
2 to raise
3 to stay
4 to find
5 advertising
6 putting
7 to begin
8 placing
9 Finding
10 to work

6 1 who your supplier is?
2 if / whether you've been offered the job yet?
3 how much the shipping cost?
4 if / whether you supply any of our competitors?
5 how long the order will take?
6 where you studied?
7 if / whether the order arrived on time?
8 how much interest the account pays?

Vocabulary

1 a) mend
2 c) fit
3 c) an overdraft
4 c) fill in
5 c) harbour
6 c) confident
7 b) loss
8 c) prevent
9 c) refund
10 c) wrapped
11 a) postcode
12 b) margins
13 a) qualifications
14 c) installation
15 a) rates
16 a) claim
17 c) penalty
18 b) join
19 b) priority
20 a) resignation
21 c) negotiate
22 a) advice
23 a) load
24 b) borrow
25 b) bossy
26 a) border
27 c) statement
28 b) withdraw
29 a) itinerary
30 b) duties
31 c) freight
32 a) vacancy
33 b) discount
34 b) budget
35 b) commission
36 c) debt
37 c) reviewed
38 a) discount
39 b) inspect
40 c) deposit
41 c) consignments
42 a) careful
43 c) funds
44 a) operator
45 a) exchanges
46 c) ferry
47 a) handed in
48 b) branches
49 c) licence
50 a) rent

Answer key (Writing)

Emails

1 a, e, c, b, d – length of message, increasingly informal terms of address (*Dear Mr Laws, Charles*), increasingly informal style (*I'll, Thanks*), increasingly informal closings (from *Yours sincerely to Thanks*).

2

openings	closings
Dear Mr Laws	Yours sincerely
Dear Charles / Joyce	Kind regards
Joyce	Regards
Nothing	All the best
	Nothing

3 1 False. Email is used for speed or convenience. Like any form of communication, the level of formality is decided by the relationship between the writer and reader.
2 Usually true, but not always.
3 Often true, but not always. (See question 1.)
4 True. When people reply to an email, they often do not use an opening – especially with very short replies.

4 Sample answers:

Dear Mrs Walters
Thanks for your email of 14 April. I'm sorry but I won't be able to attend the meeting on 9 May. The following week would be a lot better for me – could we meet then? Please let me know.
Kind regards
Francesca

Francesca
Thanks for your email. The following week is fine for me. How about 16 May? Please let me know.
Regards
Anne

Letters

1 Sample answer:

Anja Ratzenberger
Network Schweiz
Neunbrunnenstr 18
8050 Zurich
Switzerland

25 May 2011

Re: Your letter of 24 May

Dear Ms Ratzenberger

Thank you for your letter of 24 May. We would be very interested to hear more about your company and its services. Therefore, we would be very grateful if you could send us a brochure with a price list. Would it also be possible to arrange a visit some time in the week commencing 7 June?

We look forward to hearing from you.

Yours sincerely

Gill Thomson